The Bazaar

Raad Chalabi, PhD

D1798730

To order additional copies of this book, contact:
Xlibris Corporation
1-888-795-4274
www.Xlibris.com
Orders@Xlibris.com

Introduction

Tourist: I understand you live here in this Bazaar?

Ramiz: Yes I do.

Tourist: How many entrances to The Bazaar?

Ramiz: One.

Tourist: How many exists?

Ramiz: One.

Tourist: Are they the same?

Ramiz: No.

Tourist: Is there an opening and closing time?

Ramiz: Each visitor has his own opening and closing time.

Tourist: What are mine?

Ramiz: I do not know?

Tourist: Whom can I ask?

Ramiz: I do not know anybody who knows.

Tourist: You do not seem to know much about the Bazaar?

Ramiz: Does anybody know much about anything?

Tourist: I know a lot about the place where I live.

Ramiz: Satisfaction is always good.

Tourist: You mean I am deluding myself?

Ramiz: Are you?

Tourist: No I am not

Ramiz: I am happy for you.

Tourist: Do many tourists come here?

Ramiz: I know no one who is not a tourist.

Tourist: How about those who sell things here?

Ramiz: I know no one who does not sell something.

Tourist: I do not understand; how can everybody in the Bazaar be a tourist and at the same time everybody in the Bazaar is selling something?

Ramiz: I agree the Bazaar is difficult to understand.

Tourist: You live here surely you must understand?

Ramiz: Every time I think I do; I quickly find out I don't.

Tourist: Is the Bazaar that big?

Ramiz: I have not yet been to all its parts; so I do not know?

Tourist: How long have you lived here?

Ramiz: All my life.

Tourist: How old are you?

Ramiz: From my prospective as old as the Bazaar; from your prospective as old as this conversation lasts.

Tourist: I come from a place where we know time; we know size; we have allocated tasks; we have responsibilities; you on the other hand claim that in the Bazaar all this is meaningless?

Ramiz: I have made no such claim.

Tourist: You do not think that knowing your age; knowing the opening and closing time of the Bazaar; knowing who does what in the Bazaar; knowing the size of the Bazaar are important matters so that someone like you who lives in the Bazaar should know?

Ramiz: If they are important matters to you then you should of course know them.

Tourist: So your point is that they are not important to you and therefore you do not know them?

Ramiz: You asked me what I know and I told you; it seems to me that you are frustrated with the limit of my knowledge; although I think that is to your benefit.

Tourist: Why is that?

Ramiz: The Bazaar is something you experience not something you learn about from others. Walk in and reach your own conclusions.

Hammer: Where have you been? We missed you.

Drill: Some idiot in despatch sent me to a dentist by mistake.

Hammer: What happened?

Drill: I, the nurse, the dentist and two of his patients kept explaining to the Courier guy that I am a construction drill and not a dentist drill. He would not budge. Apparently he can only deliver and cannot collect.

Hammer: So what happened then?

Drill: I had to wait at the dentist clinic for two days. The courier firm then sent somebody to collect me.

Hammer: But you were away for much longer than two days.

Drill: I know. I was taken by the courier to quarantine at their main depot. Apparently I had to be inspected by the financial controller before I can be despatched back here to where I was supposed to be

1

sent in the first place. It took him two days to come, three days to issue his report, in triplicate, placing the blame for the error on the dentist for not specifying the exact type of drill he required. Therefore everybody in the courier company felt safe and no one was to blame.

Hammer: Then they delivered you here?

Drill: No. The problem became that because I spent more than three days in their depot in quarantine so somebody had to pay for my stay there. The dentist's response to their request to pay was too impolite for me to repeat but it involved me and would have caused the courier company's chairman great discomfort.

Hammer: This is all unbelievable. What happened next?

Drill: I took the initiative. I volunteered to go and spend some quality time in the supervisor's home and after four days he

delivered me here. What I do not understand is how come nobody here chased the courier when I did not arrive in the first place?

Hammer: I think they were all happy because during your absence no work was being done.

Drill: Why did the management not bring a replacement?

Hammer: The union refused because they had declared you kidnapped and allowed no other drill to benefit from your absence until you are safely returned.

Drill: How come then my union did not pursue matters with the courier company to secure my release?

Hammer: I was told they do not deal with terrorists or kidnappers. It is union policy.

Tozokhan (*hurricane)*: Stop huffing and puffing you could not even blow down a wooden hut.

Jackie (*smaller hurricane*): I suppose you are proud of your work. You destroyed more than half the seashore towns you visited.

Tozokhan: Proud no. Satisfied with the lesson I taught its people; yes.

Jackie: What lesson?

Tozokhan: Nature is too scary to trifle with. It must be taken very seriously

Jackie: Why do you think people are not taking it seriously?

Tozokhan: Because they insist on giving us hurricanes silly human names as if we are related.

Jackie: But your name is different? I have not met any human I know with such a name.

Tozokhan: That's why I only destroyed half the sea shore towns as my gesture of good will.

Moon: Tell those creatures that reside on you to stop using me as their love symbol?

Earth: Why?

Moon: On their last visit to me they jumped on my head; shoved flag up my backside and then left by farting on me.

Earth: Well are you surprised. You do not allow them to breathe you give them no water and you refused them any food.

Moon: Fine. I do not deny what I am; let them use you as a love symbol and leave me alone.

Earth: You must be joking. You complained when three people jumped on your head; I have seven billion doing that to me asking me for more water and food all the time. They cut my trees, let their factories and cars fart at me, teach their chemical plants to piss into my rivers, they interfere with my ozone defences from that burning idiot

they call the sun and to top it all they have accumulated enough nuclear gadgets to blow everything on me to pieces.

Moon: Why do you let them get away with it?

Earth: I don't. I do treat them regularly with hurricanes; earthquakes; famine, floods, and highly contagious diseases.

Moon: Are they learning to behave?

Earth: I think so; but that's what I thought about the dinosaurs and I was obviously wrong.

Moon: I really am glad I am nasty to them otherwise they would be riding me too. Tell them they could carry on using me as their love symbol as long as they do not visit me.

Mosquito 1: What's with the new antenna?

Mosquito 2: It is government issued equipment. I now work for them.

Mosquito 1: Doing what?

Mosquito 2: Collecting blood samples from suspects for DNA testing.

Mosquito 1: What kind of suspects?

Mosquito 2: The kind they cannot bring in into a police station for standard DNA testing. I fly to the unsuspecting target, get the blood sample and return to base depositing it in a specialised container.

Mosquito 1: Suppose you chose the wrong target?

Mosquito 2: Not possible. First through my antenna I receive the co-ordinates via satellite and secondly I must, once I deposit the blood of the target, proceed to repeat the exercise with at least two direct relatives. This allows my controller a means to compare and verify.

Mosquito 1: Do you get paid for that work?

Mosquito 2: Yes. Three plastic capsules of fresh goat or pig blood per target. They have also kindly allowed me to open an account in a local blood bank where I can save some of my capsules for my retirement.

Mosquito 1: How many targets do they use you for?

Mosquito 2: Well I do on average about five targets per shift except when I am on overseas assignments then I do three per shift. I do two days on one day off, plus two weeks annual holiday.

Mosquito 1: Can they use DNA acquired through you in a court case?

Mosquito 2: I do not know about that. All I know is that I had two judges as my target last week.

Dictionary: What is it that you do?

Suspicion: I create doubt and breed conspiracy theories.

Dictionary: Why?

Suspicion: Because of my religious beliefs.

Dictionary: Your religion teaches you to do that?

Suspicion: Not directly. Basically it says evil is everywhere and good is in constant battle with it. I invent scenarios that allow good to take precautions.

Dictionary: Suppose your predictions are wrong?

Suspicion: Well then it means that evil is even more devious than I imagined and I double my efforts and try harder.

Tourist: Excuse me Sir, is the Bazaar open?

Cleaner: It never closes my friend. Are you a tourist?

Tourist: Are we not all tourists in this world?

Cleaner: I meant have you travelled far to come here?

Tourist: It depends what you mean by far? If you mean airline travel time then the trip was about eight hours; if you mean culture travel time then I can only tell once my visit is complete. What is it you do here?

Cleaner: Well I usually dance with this broom that I am holding. She in appreciation of the attention I bestow upon her lets her straw skirt caress the streets of the Bazaar.

Tourist: Have you two been dancing long?

Cleaner: I for the last twenty seven years; she on the other hand has been doing it for three years only.

Tourist: What happened to your other partners?

Cleaner: The first died dancing; the second became a vacuum cleaner and emigrated while the third was too ambitious to continue dancing. She wanted a better life elsewhere. I did not stand in her way.

Tourist: You understand ambition then?

Cleaner: Of course I do. It is my ambition that kept me going all these years.

Tourist: Your ambition to do what?

Cleaner: To complete my understanding of human nature through studying in detail what people throw away in public places and what they retain for private disposal.

Tourist: Do you feel you are close to achieving your ambition?

Cleaner: No.

Tourist: Why not?

Cleaner: Many factors really. Firstly people's perception of what is of value and should be retained keeps changing; secondly people's expectations of what they may need in future keeps changing; thirdly the concept that what is public needs to be respected is eroding; fourthly what was considered as private at some earlier point ceases to be so as time passes by and fifthly new things seem to be added daily that are designed to be thrown away.

Tourist: That is a lot of variables to consider in one life-time. Why don't you limit your study to a defined period of time to reduce the effect of the change factor?

Cleaner (*smiling*): You want me to study human nature without taking change into consideration? The

whole essence of human history is that change is inevitable. How can I box my ambition by limiting myself to a period?

Tourist: But this way you would die before you would ever achieve your ambition of a full understanding of human nature through monitoring its waste disposal habits?

Cleaner: Everybody dies; in my case I would prematurely die if I have no ambition. I wake up every morning excited of the additional knowledge I will acquire during the day; spending the evening documenting what I learned and then sleep at night hoping that tomorrow would add some more. You want me to throw that away?

Tourist: But would you not want to bring your research to closure at some point to match your own life span?

Cleaner: Why? Would human nature cease to change at the day I die?

Tourist: But surely you became a cleaner because of circumstances? Therefore would you not have had other ambitions than the one you described if those circumstances were different?

Cleaner: Everybody you will meet in the Bazaar is there because of circumstances; in my case I maximised on them. I suppose you can call me lucky for finding that I was in the right place with the right job to pursue my lifelong ambitions.

Customer: Good morning.

Tailor: Good morning. How can I help you?

Customer: I have bought a cloth and wanted to have it tailored for a friend.

Tailor: Is your friend with you?

Customer: No he is in a far away country.

Tailor: In that case I am sorry I cannot help you.

Customer: I do have his measurements because I expected that would be a problem.

Tailor: That is not the problem; without meeting him I cannot tailor what is suitable for him. I am proud of my work and to do something not to my highest standards will trouble me.

Customer: How will meeting him help you?

Tailor: We arrive to this world naked and when we leave it is irrelevant to

us what we wear. Therefore our clothes reflect what we are in the in-between. This is too short a time to waste wearing clothes that do not reflect the true us. Unless I meet him I would not know his true nature and would therefore waste my valuable time producing a garment that was not suitably created for him.

Customer: But you get paid any way?

Tailor: If all you want is a garment to give as a present then I suggest you visit the multi-story store in the middle of the bazaar. You can buy clothes off the shelf there for the same price it would have cost you to tailor the garment. That way you can give him two gifts: the cloth and a tailored garment. You would be happy for exceeding your gift quota; your friend would be happy knowing that you remembered him and brought him two gifts instead of one and I would be happy because I did not deviate from my work principles.

Customer: So if I understand you correctly unless a client comes to you himself you will not make any garments for him.

Tailor: You are partly correct. It is not the coming to me that matters it is my knowledge of him that is critical. In tailoring a garment I am giving a part of myself to somebody; I am not willing to do it without knowing that person and knowing that what I created for him matches the image I have in my mind as to how he should be dressed.

Customer: Suppose after all that effort he did not like what you did. What happens then?

Tailor: Nothing. I keep the garment; he keeps his money and is free to seek alternative tailors.

Customer: What would happen to the garment?

Tailor: It will wait until a suitable client shows up.

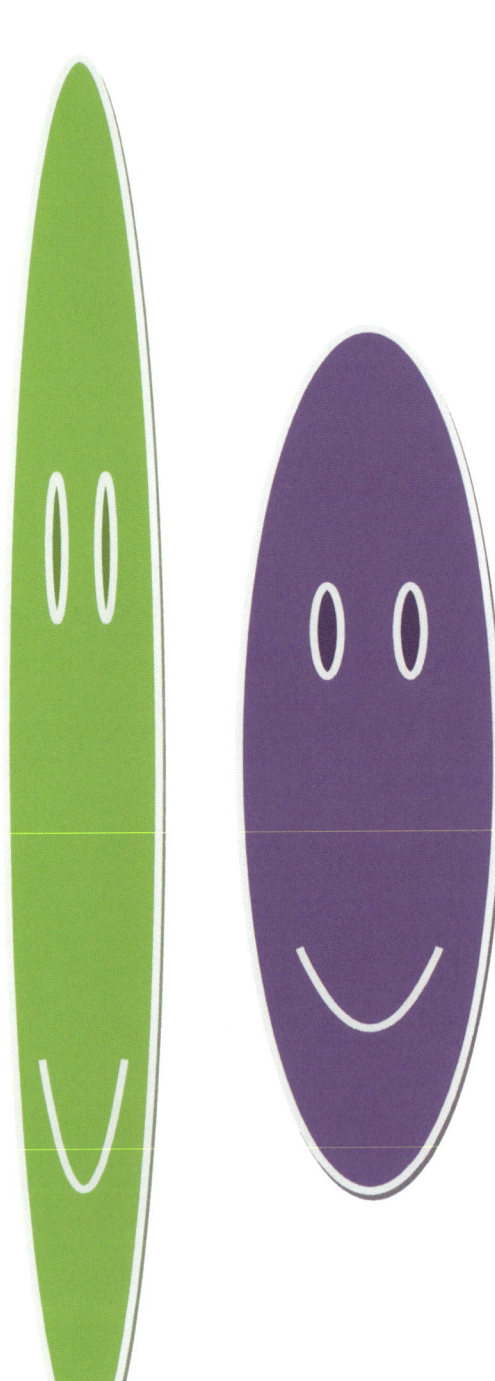

Customer: How do you know one would?

Tailor: Two reasons. One: people think they are different and unique but they are not and two: garments by their very nature can be adjusted.

Customer: Do you end up with any dead stock?

Tailor: No. I am a good reader of personalities.

Customer: How about fashion. It changes and what could have been suitable last year or the year before might not be suitable today?

Tailor: People's personalities, once they are formed, never change. My garments are designed to match the personality not to imitate a trend.

Customer: But all designers say the same thing?

Tailor: True. You and others then have the freedom to choose which designer will clothe you. This choice makes you who you are. No one

should be allowed to steal away your freedom of choice not me not anybody.

Customer: But are you not overestimating the importance of clothes?

Tailor: Elegance and beauty are never overestimated. They cause an inner thrill within the fabric of the human soul just like music and poetry. Instead of a brush and canvas I paint with a needle and thread.

Customer: Thank you for your time.

Tailor 2: Sir, I could not help but overhear your conversation in the shop next door. Please come in. I will be more than happy to tailor for you the garment you want from the cloth you already have.

Customer: Are you not bothered that it might not fit the personality of my friend?

Tailor 2: If every tailor thinks and behaves like my neighbour half the

world would be naked and the other half would spend their time asking psychiatrists what tailors they should use.

Customer: So you view clothes as a commodity?

Tailor 2: Of course. It is something we need. It should be comfortable, practical and affordable to the many.

Customer: You give me the feeling that in an ideal scenario we would all dress the same?

Tailor 2: Some of the people we most respect and care for in society do; nurses, soldiers, school children, doctors, firemen, policemen. The fact that they dress the same does not make them any less individual. They are who they are by what they do and how they think not by what they wear.

Customer: But they do not wear their uniforms when they are not on duty?

Tailor 2: That only means they do not want to be on duty twenty four hours a day.

Customer: But an entire industry has been created based on the fact that people want to wear different clothes? How could that have happened if people did not need to feel different through the clothes they wear?

Tailor 2: I do not argue that the need to be different is a true reflection of human nature. My argument is that clothes may be used as a means to say something your personality on its own is unable to say. Sooner or later once you open your mouth you are their naked for all to see. Invest in what enhances your personality not what disguises its reality. In any case you differentiate a general from a private by the stars or stripes on his shoulder not by any change in their uniform.

Customer: But beauty is very fulfilling? First impressions do matter?

Tailor 2: Discipline, team-spirit and equality are also forms of beauty enhanced by uniform dress. In any case no matter how you dress what is ugly you cannot change it. All you can do is mask it for a while.

Customer: But why not let the ugly feel beautiful for a short time?

Tailor 2: But your question favours my approach. Would you want one ugly person to feel beautiful for a short time with the purchase of an expensive one off designer dress, or fifty ugly people to feel beautiful for a short time with not so exclusive and expensive a dress?

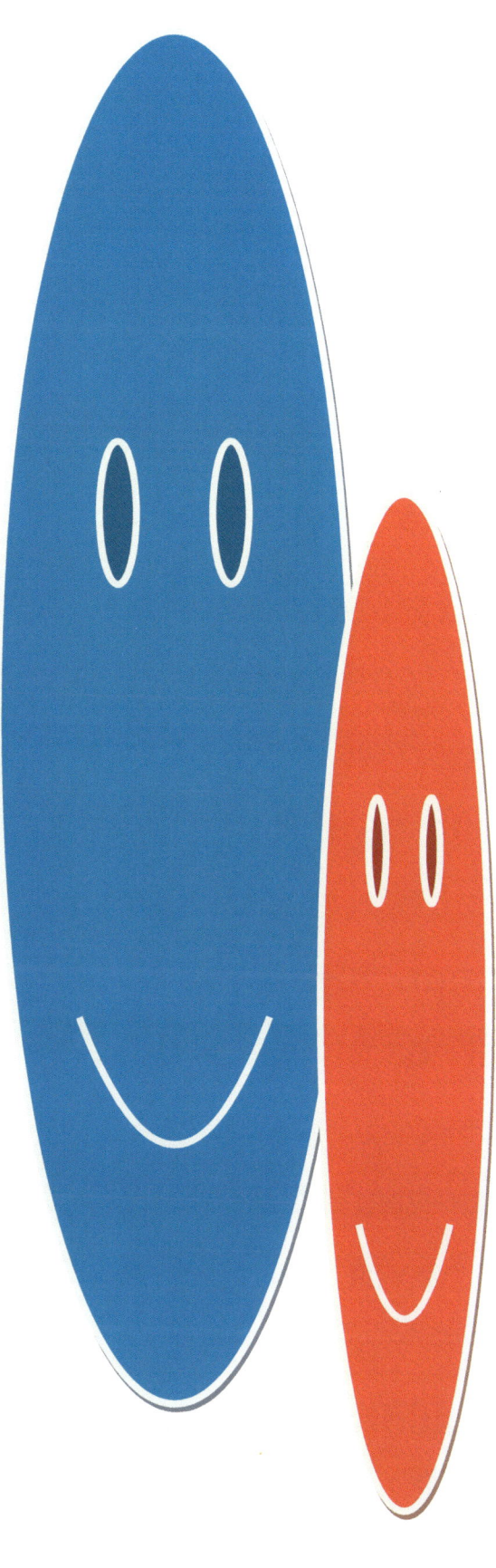

Carpet Seller: Good morning; how can I help you?

Economist: Do you sell fitted carpets or Persian rugs?

Carpet Seller: I sell both. My job is to meet your needs whatever they are.

Economist: But do you have a preference?

Carpet Seller: In terms of what I sell, no; it terms of what I buy for myself, yes.

Economist: I was talking to your neighbouring shops and one tailor specialises in exclusive designer garments and the other adopts the "pile them high and sell them cheap" philosophy; hence my question about your preference.

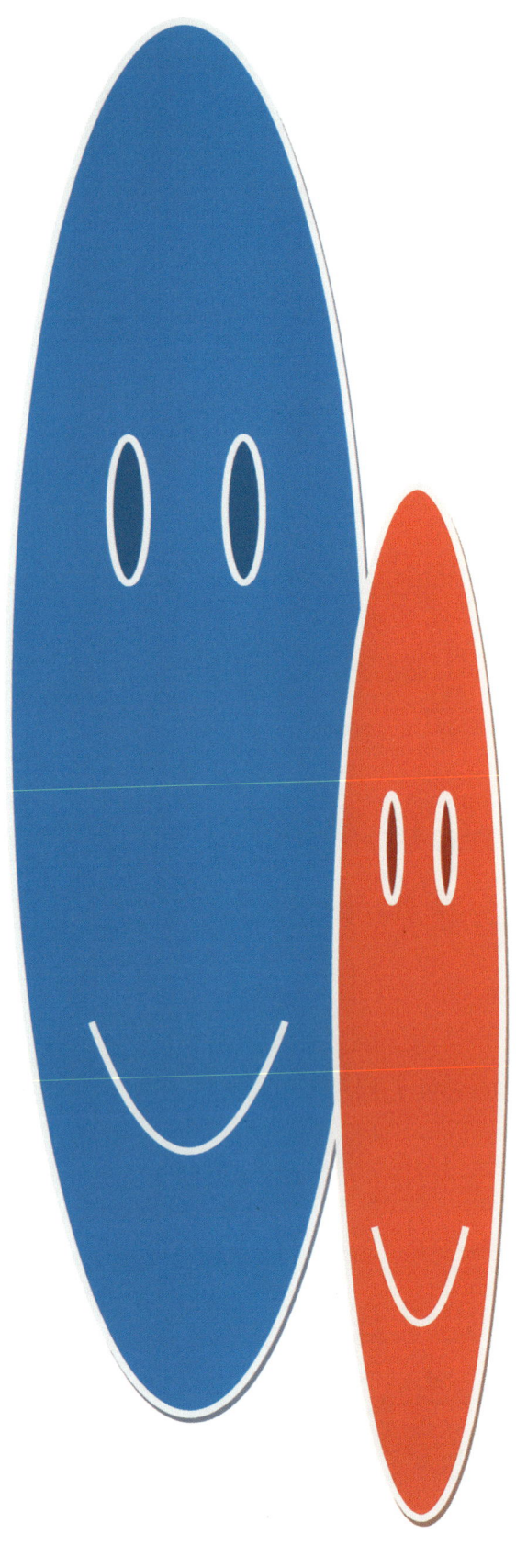

Carpet Seller: I do not sell philosophy I sell carpets. Expensive Persian rugs take years to manufacture, are beautiful to look at and appreciate in value with time. Fitted carpets sell by the meter can be regularly changed and you need not worry about theft and damage. Therefore if you appreciate beauty, believe that a traditional industry which is hundreds of years old should be preserved, you are interested in demonstrating your wealth and you are keen to die leaving an appreciating asset to your children then buying such rugs seems logical. If on the other hand you are practical, you believe

that wealth should whisper, you do not think that people should spend years of their life weaving carpet threads for you to step on, and you believe that inheritance provision is a consequence and not a duty then opt for machine manufactured fitted carpets.

Economist: What do you have at home?

Carpet Seller: This shop is my home. If you mean what I bought for the place I sleep and eat in the answer is fitted carpets everywhere except my wife's and my bedroom. There I have two of the most expensive Persian rugs.

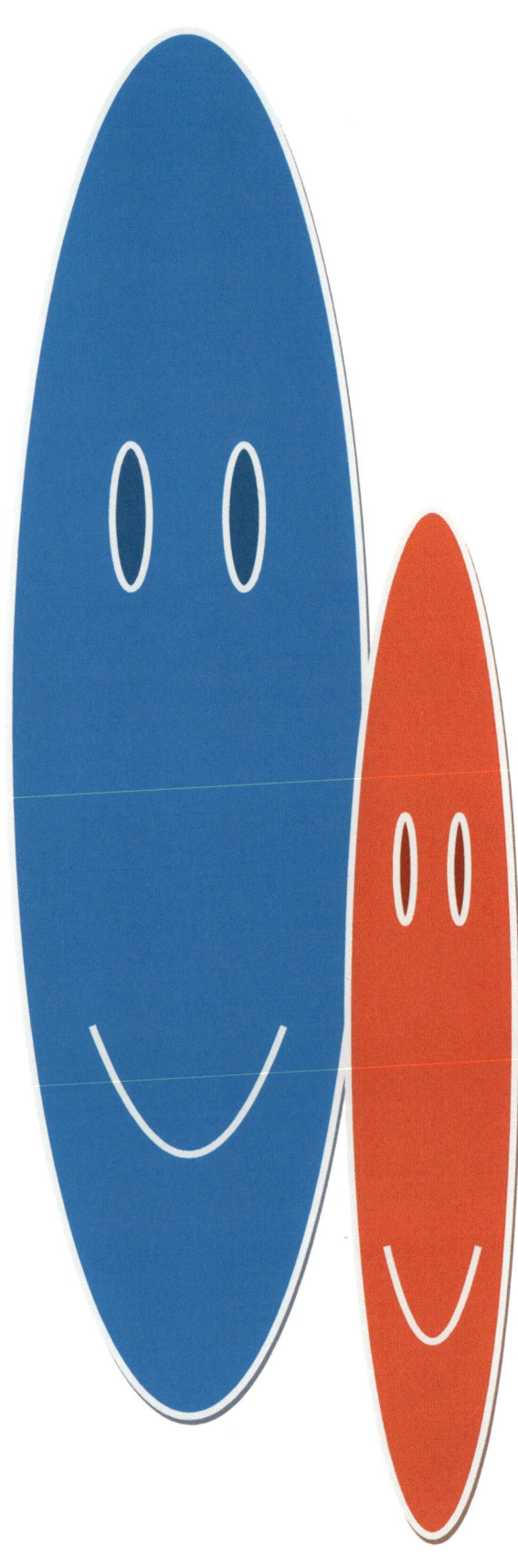

Economist: How can your place of work be your home?

Carpet Seller: I open at seven in the morning to capture the early trade and close at nine in the evening so as not to lose the evening trade. I have lunch at the premises delivered from a local restaurant in the company of fellow shop owners. I have dinner at ten in the evening with my wife and go to bed one hour later. You tell me which is my home?

Economist: You do that by choice?

Carpet Seller: Of course. Every one you will meet in the Bazaar does what he does by choice.

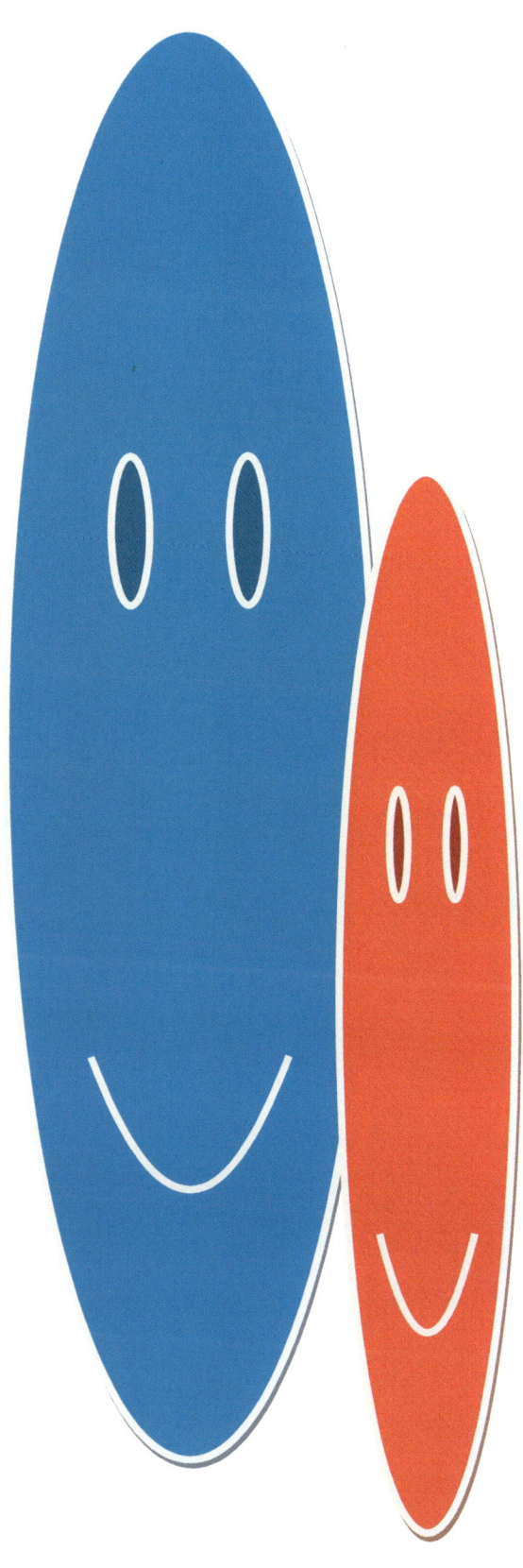

Economist: But that way you do not spend time with your family?

Carpet Seller: Time is relative my friend. Think back of every person who was close to you from your childhood. You will remember one or two incidents that happened to you with that person. This memory is not measured by the time it took for the incident to happen but by the impact it had on you. Spending time with someone is not an accountancy issue or an obligation that must be met; it is a very valuable event that must be done exclusively by choice and which should be carefully planned and leave an

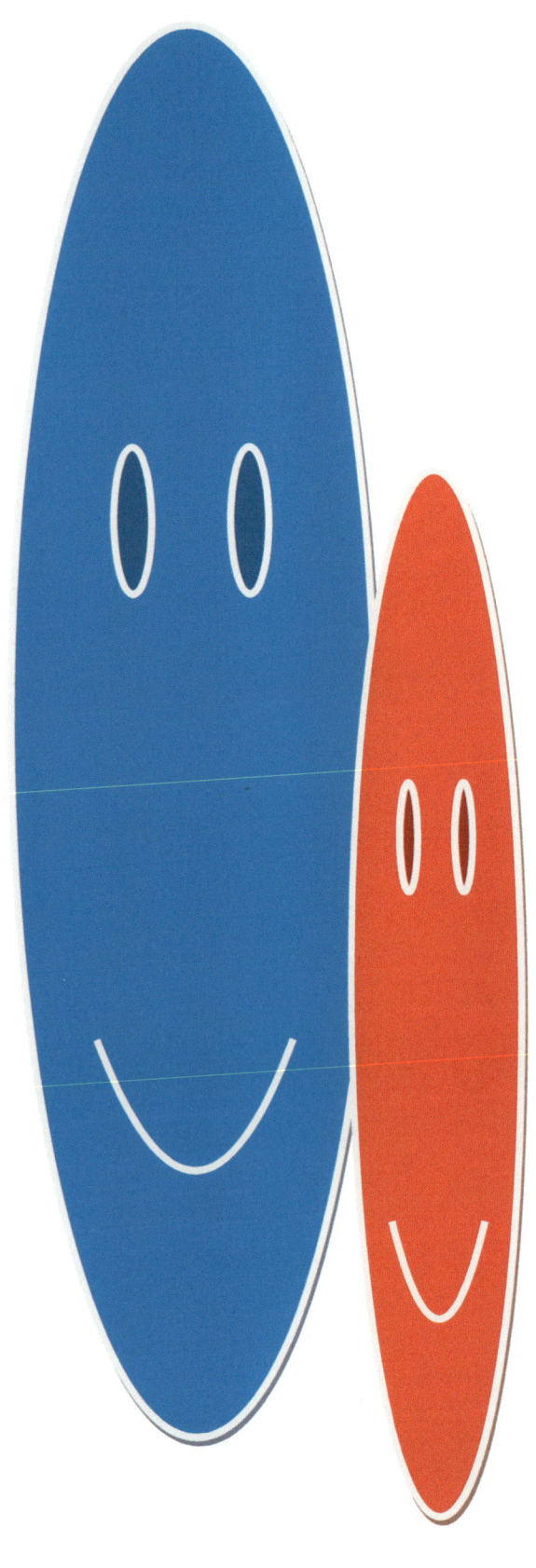

everlasting impact. It is the variety of such incidents which measure the quality of life.

Economist: What motivates you to invest so much of your time in the shop? Is it money?

Carpet Seller: Money is just a measuring tool. It is the thrill of the sale that motivates me. The buyer's money represents the non-replaceable hours and days of his life he invested to acquire it. When he purchases with it something, I predicted someone like him would want, a satisfying event happens; the time I invest in my shop is to collect such memorable events.

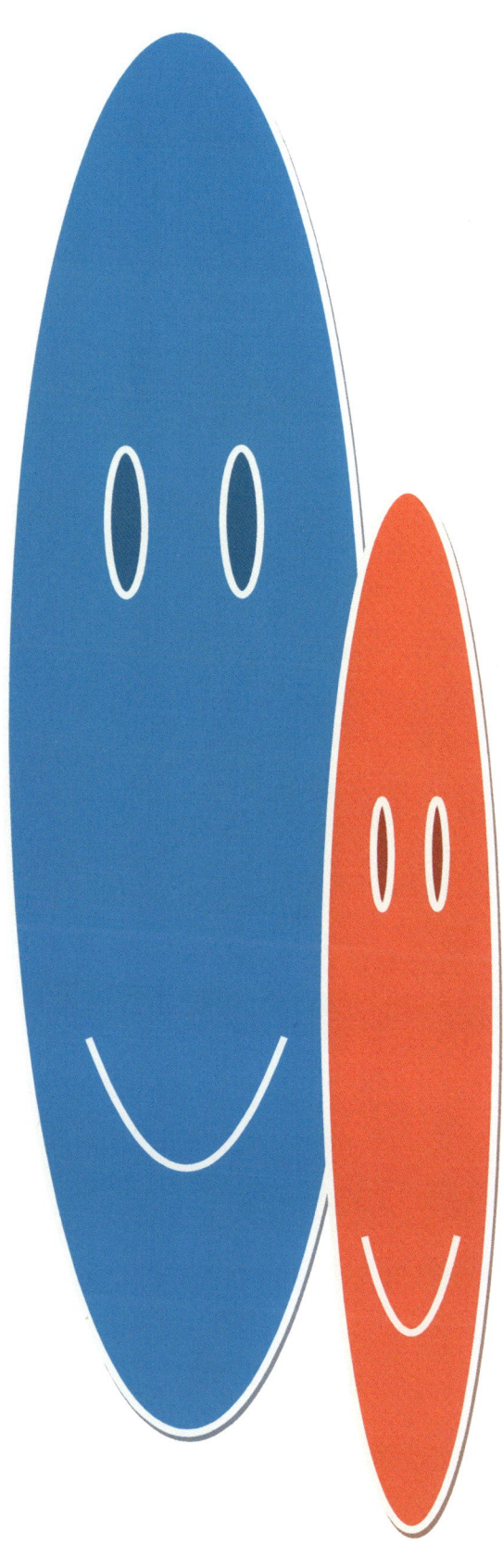

Economist: But this would have occurred through any selling process; why carpets?

Carpet Seller: Circumstances created this opportunity. I maximised on it. To dwell on the details of these circumstances is pointless since no two people would ever walk an identical path.

Economist: But a man's history is important.

Carpet Seller: Yes the history of what he has achieved is very important; the history prior to commencing his productive life is not his; and is therefore gossip.

Economist: Do you expect your children to follow your path?

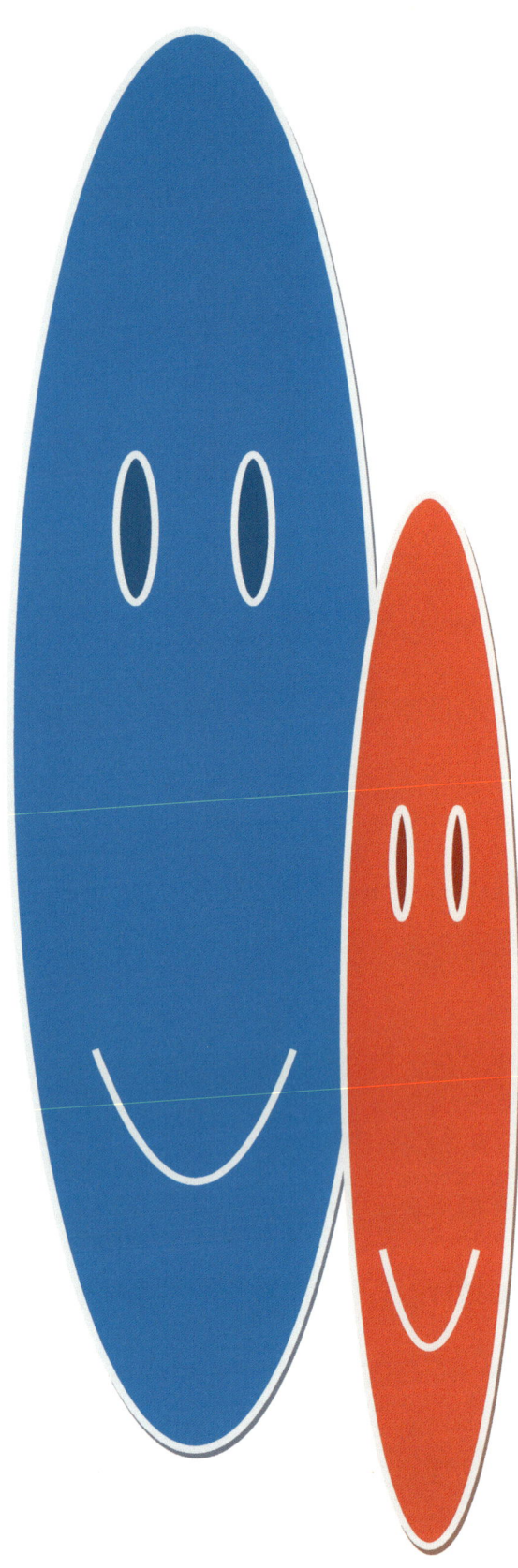

Carpet Seller: If I do I would be a bad father; if I don't then I am not human.

Economist: I understand the second part of your answer but not the first.

Carpet Seller: If I had educated my children correctly, installed in them a strong sense of freedom, helped them harness their will-power, exposed them to all possible options and then allowed them to freely choose; what right would I have to expect anything as regards what they would become?

Economist: So you do not consider them as a continuation of yourself?

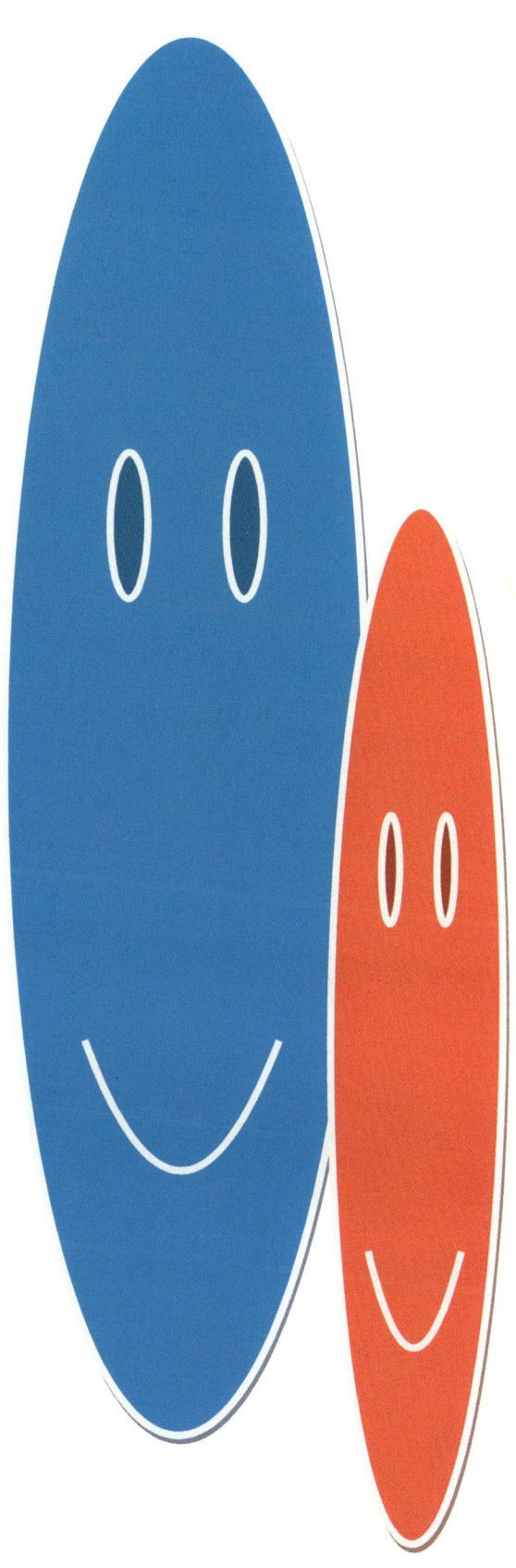

Carpet Seller: It will be a sad day if ever I thought I own them or made them feel they owe me.

Economist: Does their Mother feel the same?

Carpet Seller: I do not know what anyone feels. All I know is what people say they feel. In the case of my wife she wants them around her all the time. After all they were once part of her.

Economist: Thank you for a fascinating talk. I am sorry I did not buy a carpet from you.

Carpet Seller: It is amazing. I sold you nothing and yet I feel as if I did.

Visitor (*talking to the translator*): Please thank our host for the welcoming present he gave my wife.

Translator (*talking to the host*): He thanks you for welcoming his wife.

Host (*to translator*): Please advise him that it was a pleasure to have him and his wife as our guests.

Translator (*to visitor*): He says it was a pleasure for him to have your wife.

Visitor (*angrily to translator*): This is an insult to my honour. Tell him that immediately.

Translator (*to host*): He said it was his honour.

Host (*to translator*): But he looks very angry. Maybe he expected a bigger gift. Please tell him that I

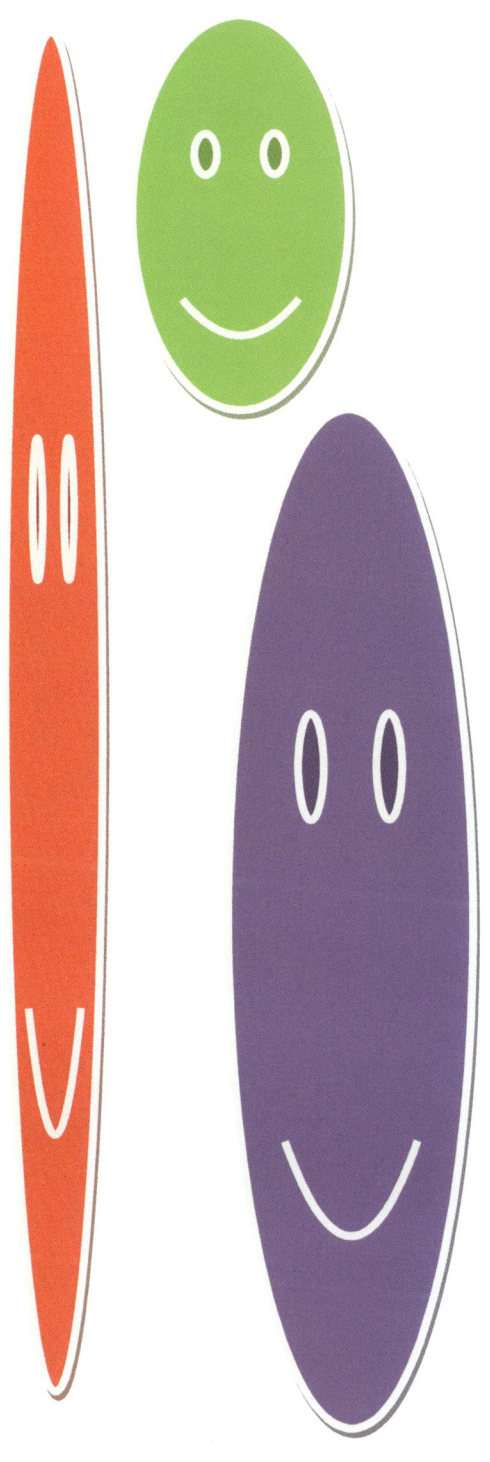

will be delighted to have him and his wife to visit me again.

Translator (*to visitor*): He said he will have your wife again.

(*Visitor left after kicking the coffee table*).

Host *(to translator)*: What happened? What did I do which was wrong?

Translator (*to host*): Your mistake was to insist on paying me a flat rate for my translation work instead of paying me on the basis of the number of words translated.

Host: Why would that make him angry and cause him to leave like this?

Translator: Maybe because he felt you attached no real value to each word you say to him.

Friend 1: Is it true your wife is divorcing you?

Friend 2: Yes.

Friend 1: Why?

Friend 2: She says I have no ambition; I am stupid and I think that life's only purpose is to get drunk.

Friend 1: But you were like this when she married you. You have not changed. Why is she objecting now?

Friend 2: She says because circumstances changed.

Friend 1: What circumstances?

Friend 2: The factory that I inherited from my father is now in her name.

Friend 1: How did that happen?

Friend 2: I sold it to her for one pound on a previous occasion

when she had threatened me with a divorce.

Friend 1: Any decent divorce lawyer will get you at least fifty percent of its value under any settlement.

Friend 2: That is not possible.

Friend 1: Why not?

Friend 2: I had signed for her an "I owe you" receipt, in the presence of two witnesses, for an amount equal to half the value of the factory.

Friend 1: Why did you do that?

Friend 2: It was after she had threatened me again with divorce a few months after the first threat.

Friend 1: What do you plan to do now?

Friend 2: Get drunk.

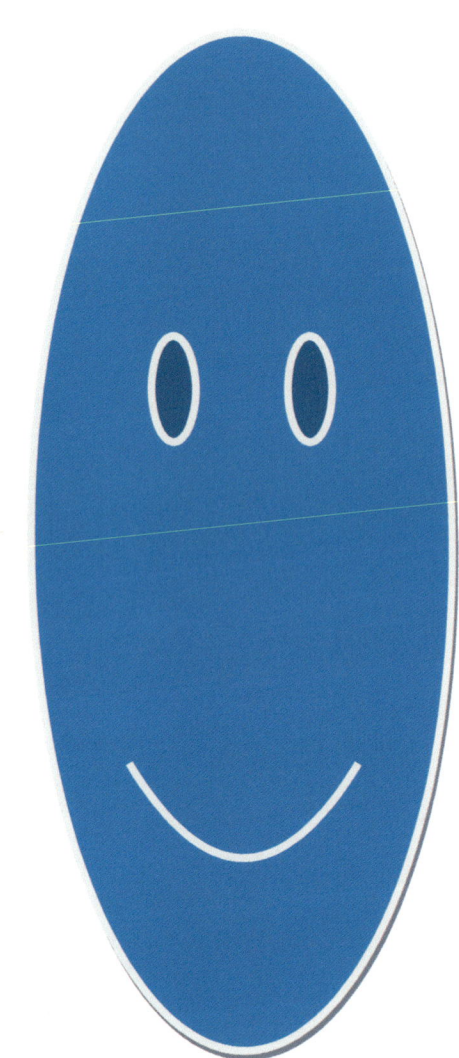

Mop: Hurry up and empty your-self the new inspector is arriving soon on a surprise inspection.

Waste Basket: What's so special about him?

Mop: His nick name is "slash and dash". He enters a room and if it is not perfect he will replace all its appliances and move to the next room.

Waste Basket: But I am too full to be able to empty myself before his arrival.

Mop: You will get us all in trouble. I have never seen anybody who eats everything they throw at him like you do.

Waste Basket: For someone who spends her life licking floors you are not qualified to criticise me.

Mop: If we spend our time exchanging insults we will both suffer.

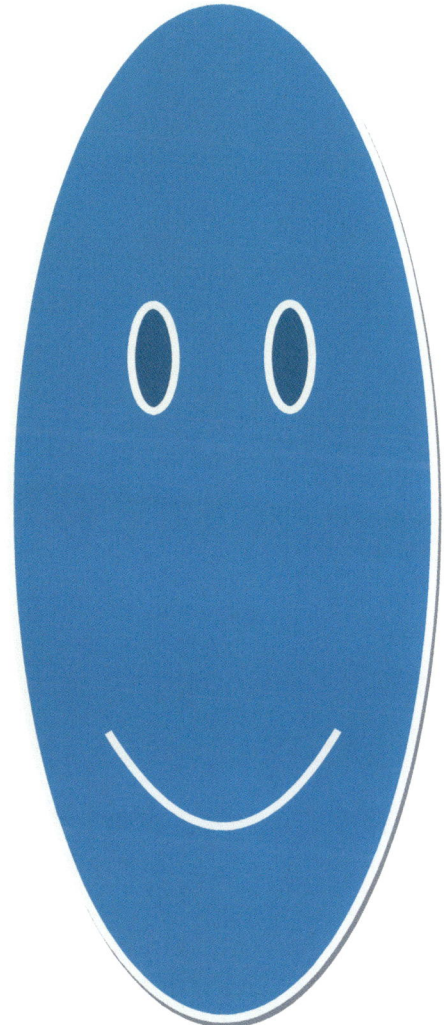

Waste Basket: How come you know that the inspector is arriving when it is supposed to be a surprise and secret visit?

Mop: Stop being silly. One of my sisters works in his office.

Waste Basket: But I have a cousin who works there and he did not know?

Mop: My sister moves around and can see things while they still are on his desk; your cousin on the other hand, who sits in a corner, will only see the papers after the event.

Waste Basket: Well my handler is away visiting her sick daughter; so I cannot be emptied. Where is your handler?

Mop: Having coffee I think.

Waste Basket: She obviously cannot empty me otherwise we will have union trouble.

Mop: So what do we do?

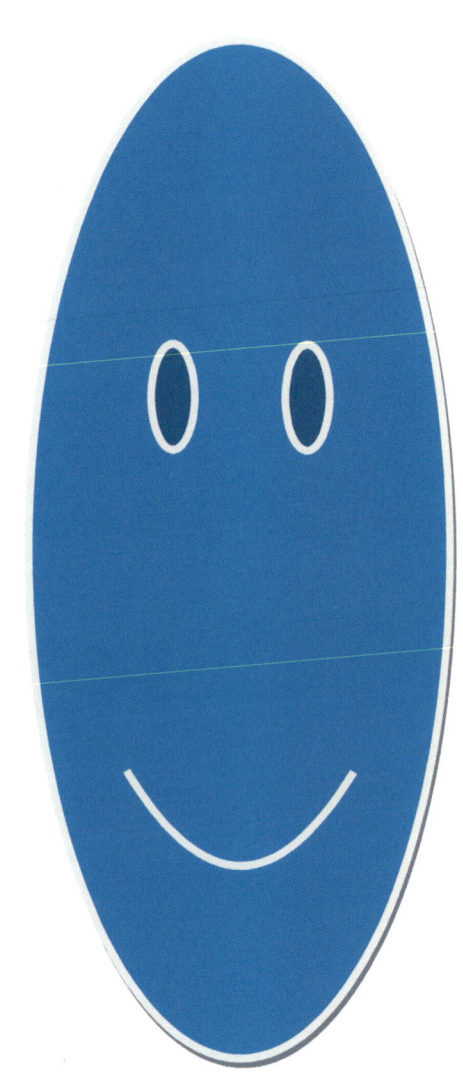

Waste Basket: If you cannot solve a problem confuse those who can expose it.

Mop: What do you mean?

Waste Basket: We tackle the inspector and distract him with our only weapon.

Mop: What weapon?

Waste Basket: The fact that we know in advance of his surprise inspection which is supposed to be secret.

Mop: What do you suggest Mr. Mastermind?

Waste Basket: You make your handler stand at the front gate with a placard that reads: "Mr. Inspector we know about your surprise visit; your office leeks."

Mop: Will that stop him coming into our room?

Waste Basket: I think so. Even if he does come into the room his report will be of no value.

Mop: Why?

Waste Basket: Because it was not a surprise visit, as it should be, and therefore all what he sees and reports on could be argued by us that it was staged.

Mop: But one would stage matters to meet the inspection criteria; in our case that would not be so.

Waste Basket: On the contrary; we would argue that we do not approve of "leeks" because they undermine an inspector's ability to do his job. Therefore we staged things to our detriment to highlight that issue. We are honest and do not approve of deception.

Mop: How come somebody like you can be so Machiavellian?

Waste Basket: As you said about my cousin, "I see the papers after the event" so I, unlike him, became a student of history. Human nature has a talent for repeating its behaviour when events are stacked

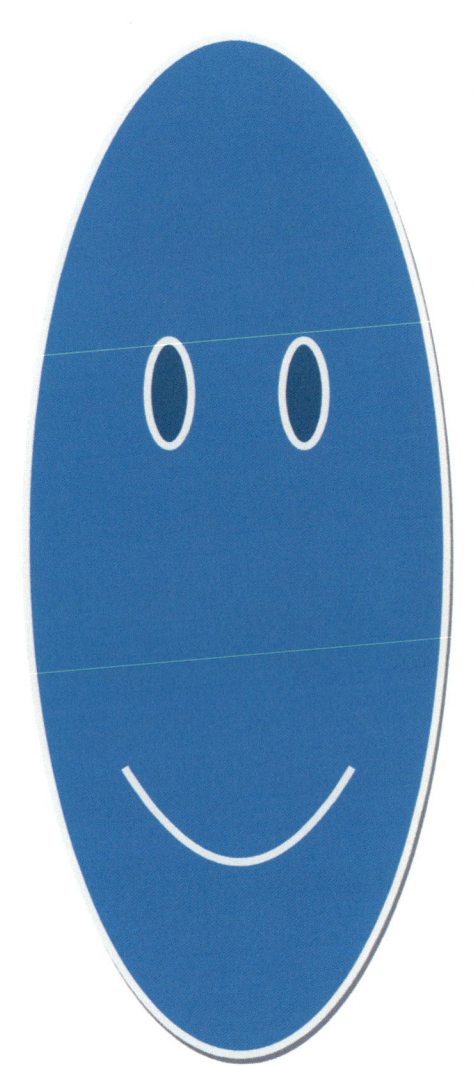

in a certain way. All I do is stage the scene and allow people to naturally behave.

Mop: I drip water in admiration; but tell me with all this obvious talent why do you still need a handler?

Waste Basket: This is the internal question that faced many great people. In that sense I share my predicament with such humans. What the mind can imagine and desire to implement is rarely matched by what the body can deliver.

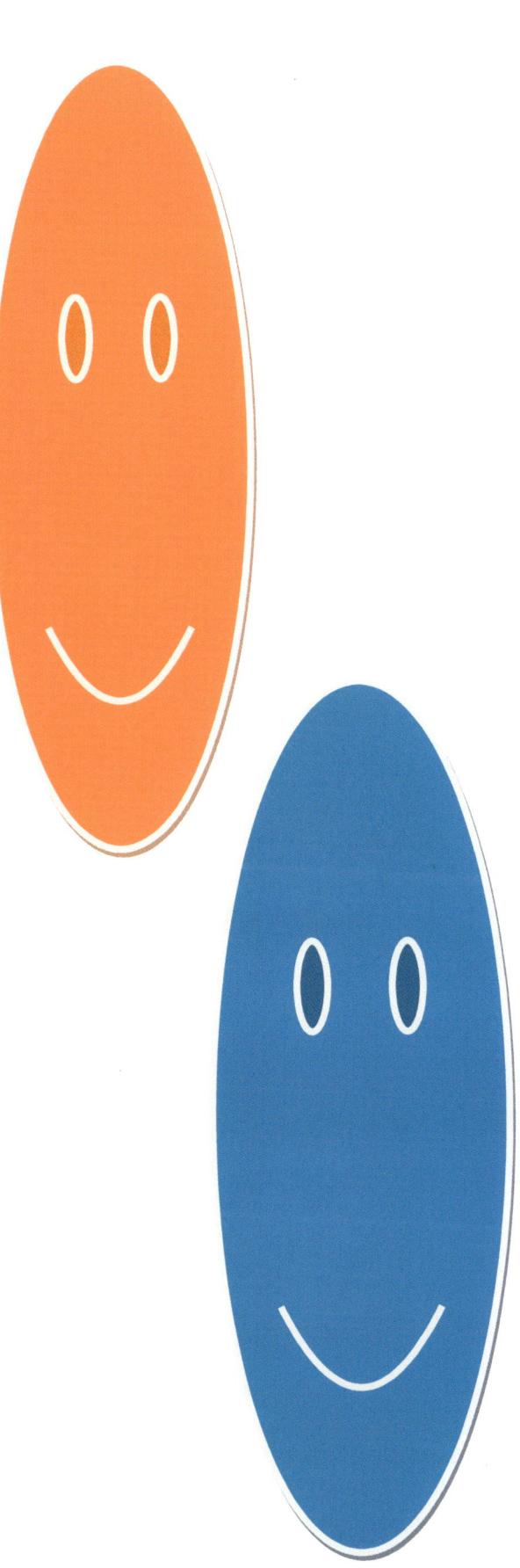

Listener: Yesterdays story was very painful to all those that listened to it. I hope you will tell us today a more joyful tale.

Story Teller: It is easier to convey sadness than it is to convey joy. There is a greater abundance of pain and hence it is easier for my listeners to identify with what I say.

Listener: But they come to you to make them happy not to remind them of reality.

Story Teller: I reflect what they feel; If I create what they have never experienced I will lose their attention and with it my job.

Listener: But they do have incidents of happiness and joy. Why does not your story telling build on that?

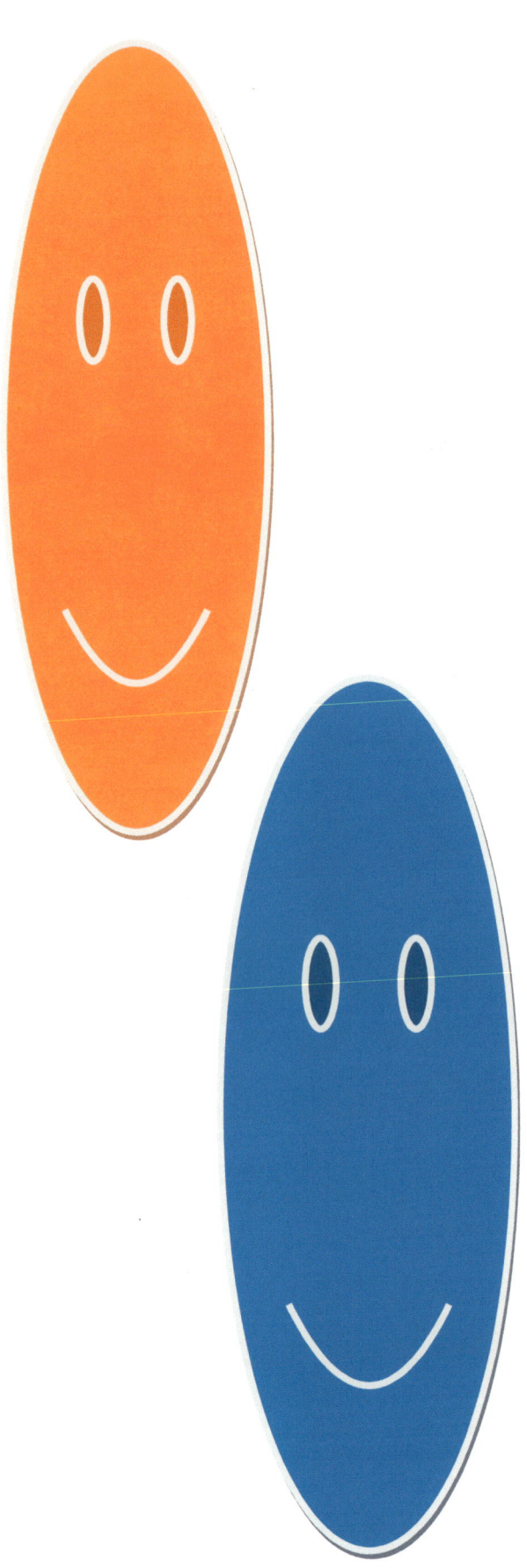

Story Teller: I cater for a large audience and on average they have been slapped around by reality more times than they have been caressed by her. Since I have to tickle the largest shared memory then pain becomes an obvious choice for my story.

Listener: But that is the easy option. To promote the lowest common denominator in anything is to deny your listeners the right to aspire for a better living. Your job is to show new horizons unless you do not know any?

Story Teller: You want a teacher go to school; you want horizons listen to your so called leaders; you want to feel happy, get drunk; you want a non violent release for your emotional frustrations then come to me. I will then tell you a sad story that

makes yours appear insignificant, you then go home feeling better until you meet tomorrow.

Listener: But life is not all misery and frustration?

Story Teller: I fully agree. All I do is cater for my own audience .I am sure many other story tellers tell different stories full of love and happiness that touches their audience's shared memories.

Listener: But what makes your audience different from theirs?

Story Teller: if I knew that they would not be my audience; neither would I be their story teller.

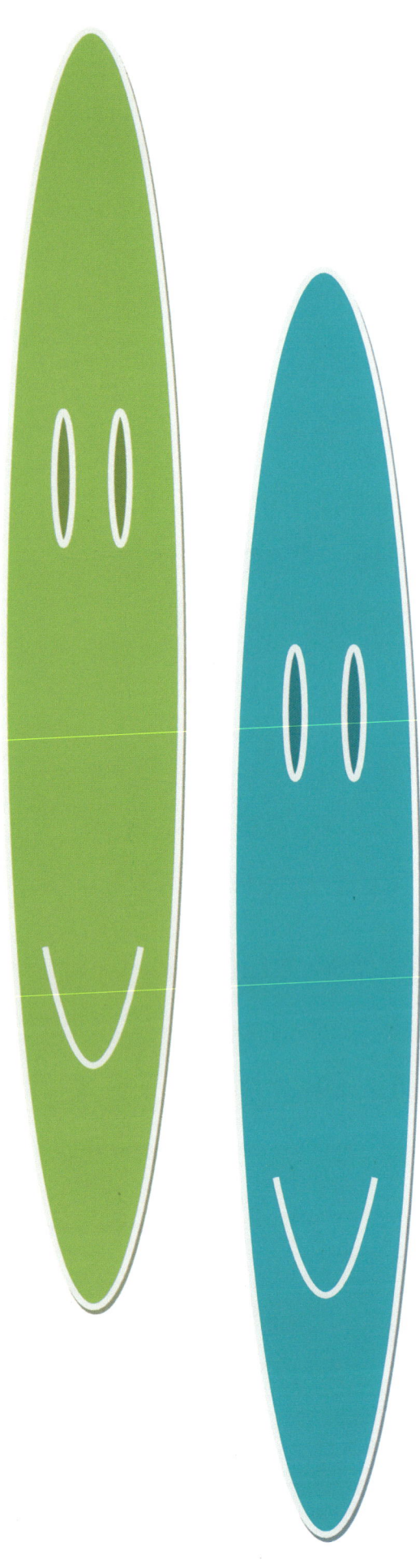

Tourist: I understand you are travelling on the road to tranquillity through science. May I join you on part of your trip?

Scientist: Why do you wish to do so?

Tourist: I have an option pursue that road through belief or through science and I wanted to sample each before I decide.

Scientist: I am not sure the two roads are exclusive but this is for you to decide. All I can do is explain my settled judgment on the current state of affairs.

Tourist: I have noticed two key phrases in what you said that make me think you want to hedge your bets in what you are about to say.

Scientist: I assume you mean the phrases "settled judgement" and "current state"?

Tourist: Yes they do not sound too scientific to me.

Scientist: It is critical to appreciate that science is based on carrying out controlled experiments that produce data. Once sufficient people have repeated those experiments generating very similar data then the scientific community accepts this as a fact and it becomes a "settled judgement". However these facts then must then be explained by a theory which allows us to predict these facts from basic assumptions. These theories are continuously fine tuned or in many cases partially or completely replaced by new ones hence my use of the phrase "current state". Science never stops.

Tourist: I am told that the process of life was kick started

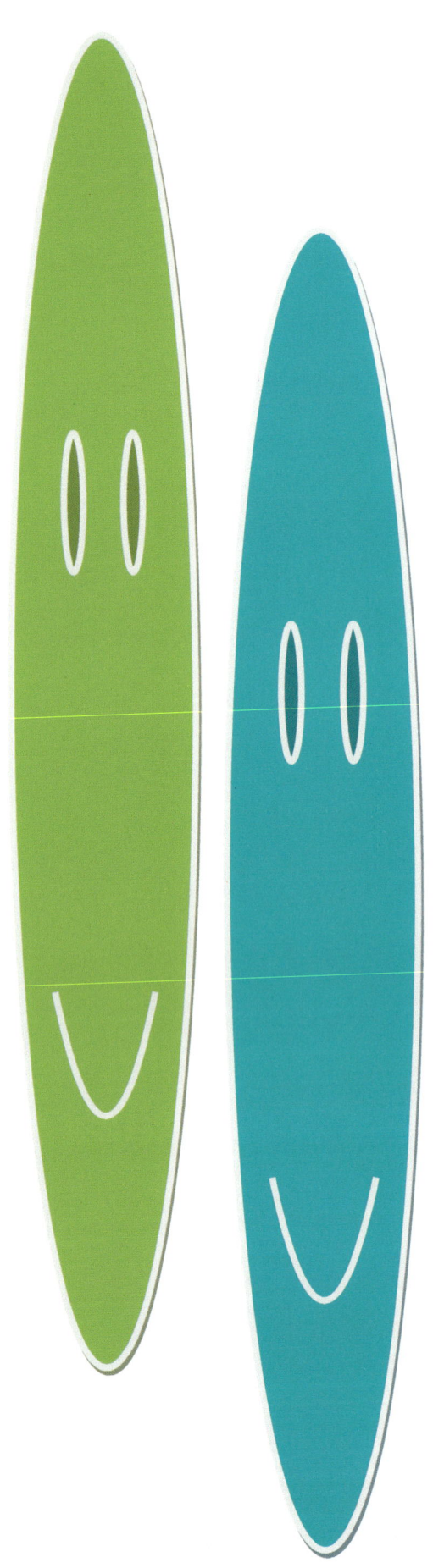

by an event called the big bang whose consequences were the formation of this universe.

Scientist: Billions of years ago a dot of concentrated energy blew up; the energy converted into discrete particles which upon cooling due to expansion condensed into heavier and heavier composites.

Tourist: Where did it come from and what caused this so called dot to blow up?

Scientist: We do not know.

Tourist: What do we know?

Scientist: We do not understand the early microseconds after the big bang, but through the theory of relativity, we can explain the process by which galaxies, stars and planets were subsequently formed and how they behave.

Tourist: Does that theory also explain the behaviour of elementary particles like electrons?

Scientist: No their behaviour is explained by a theory called quantum mechanics which is also backed by experimental facts.

Tourist: Are those two theories not linked?

Scientist: As things stand they do not seem to be; but attempts are continuing to unify them.

Tourist: Do I gather from what you said that there is nothing unique about the formation of the Earth?

Scientist: Earth is just another planet from millions and millions of others. As to its environment in terms of water, air and the

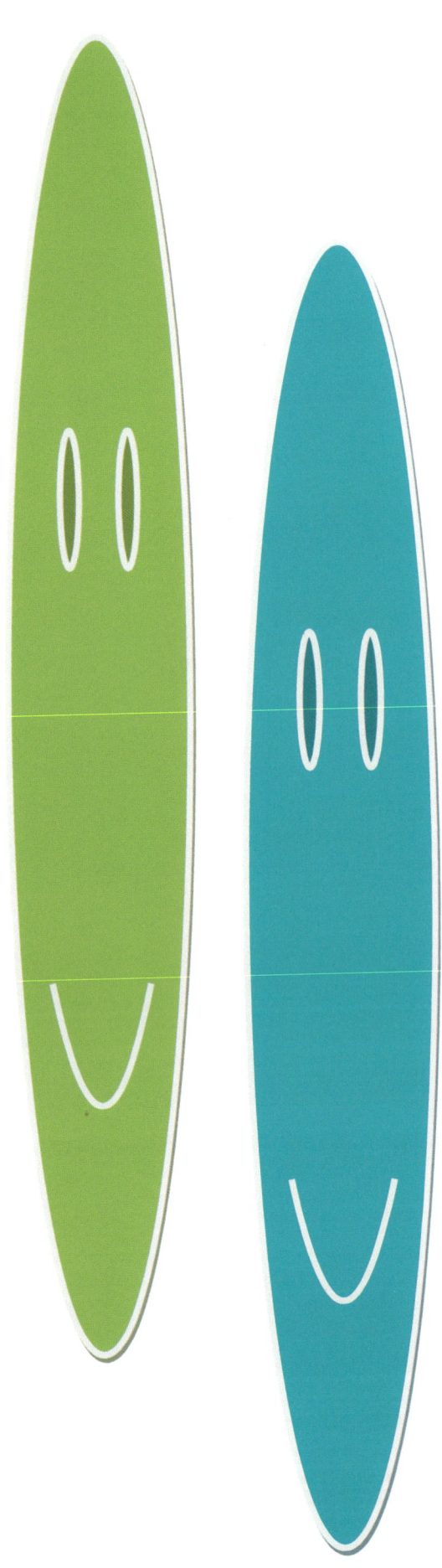

existence of life we have as yet not identified any equivalent.

Tourist: What about humans and their evolution?

Scientist: We understand the chemistry of how atoms react to form molecules. We understand how molecules interact to form composites. We understand why such molecules are biologically active. What we cannot do as yet is turn the correctly assembled ingredients to a living organism. In summary we understand to a large extent the life process but cannot as yet artificially create it.

Tourist: This big bang to humans seems a very complex process. Is that a fair conclusion?

Scientist: Very much so. A more puzzling aspect of this process is that when it is analysed mathematically it seems highly

dependent on a set of exact values without which the process could not have happened.

Tourist: So from what you say I conclude that we have no understanding of why the big bang happened; what kick starts life and why we have not as yet found life elsewhere. These are very big gaps in our overall knowledge. How do you cope with this?

Scientist: There is too much intellectual beauty and elegance in the big bang to human story to permit me to believe that it is just an accident. However; certainty, at our current state of knowledge, is not an option. I therefore choose to keep an open mind.

Tourist: But this incomplete knowledge can leave a vacuum

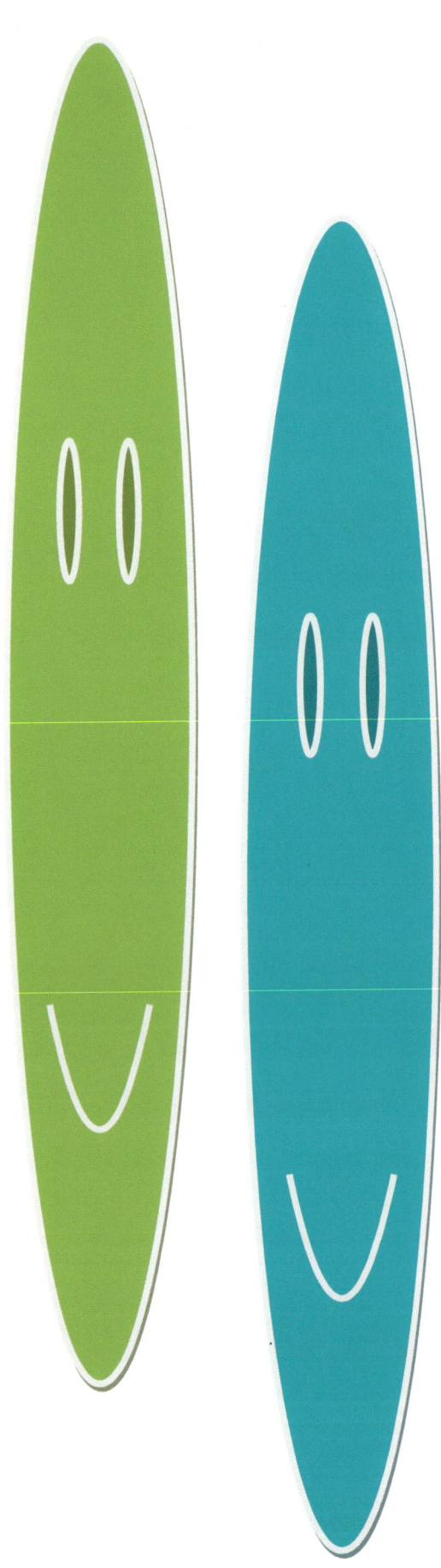

that is probably best satisfied through religion. Is that not the case?

Scientist: Beliefs, religious or otherwise, to complete the picture, seem to be a human psychological need; I certainly cannot be a stumbling block for anybody who seeks that option.

Tourist: Do you promote any belief?

Scientist: I only promote the belief that we should always seek knowledge; and that we should not actively create doubt in the minds of those who find satisfaction in any religious belief they choose to pursue as long as it does not harm others.

Tourist: Are you saying to me that everyone should find his own answer?

Scientist: It is up to you to conclude what you want from what I said.

Tourist: But it is more comforting to be part of a group otherwise life will be very cold.

Scientist: I suppose it depends on the group and what they are doing.

Tourist: You have not quenched my thirst as far as a complete scientific story is concerned?

Scientist: How would I be able to quench your thirst when I am still thirsty? All I can do is share with you what little water I have.

Tourist: So where does the tranquillity come from?

Scientist: From the knowledge that you are travelling towards it.

Zero: Hi; where have you been?

Equal: Very busy. Any time there is a gathering or departure of numbers I am called in to mediate.

Zero: I am busy too you know.

Equal: Don't give me that. You are only called in when the groups of numbers cancel each other.

Zero: You seem to forget that any number in the world has the option to include me among its team. I therefore do not accept that I am less busy than you.

Equal: That's another thing. I am always invited alone to any mathematical gathering. You on the other hand can be joined by many of your brothers and sisters.

Zero: You call that an advantage. The other day several of my brothers and I attempted to convince the number seven that he should learn to share; when we asked him to divide with his neighbour , the number six, he dumped his leftovers on us.

Equal: What did you do?

Zero: We forced him to divide the number twenty two which made him very dizzy and sick.

Equal: I hear that the number three is another one of those prima donnas.

Zero: Yes I made him marry one of my sisters and when they multiplied their offspring was one of us.

Equal: How come nobody wants you on your own like they do with me? Yet they are happy to welcome you as a part of a team of numbers provided you do not head the team. Are you that boring on your own?

Zero: I do not know about boring I certainly feel worthless when I am alone. I suppose by nature I am a social animal not a loner like you are.

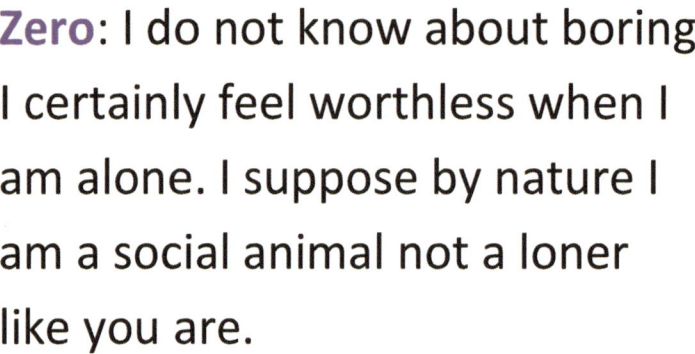

Equal: I hear you create a very big fuss when any number tries to divide by you.

Zero: I refuse to let people sit on top of me. They can stand by me but not on top of me. Pass that on to any number you meet who invites you to mediate.

Equal: It creates problems for me too; as I can never give an answer as to what would happen when numbers do sit on you.

Man 1: I lost my glass eyes?

Man 2: You mean eye glasses?

Man 1: I sorry am; I words reverse.

Man 2: Is that an illness?

Man 1: Yes.

Man 2: Is there a cure?

Man 1: Stand I down upside.

Man 2: I am sorry for you.

Man 1: You thank.

Man 2: Yes I thank God it is not contagious.

Man 1: Do how know you?

Man 2: Mean you is it?

Man 1: Yes.

Man 2: ***~****

Scarf: Why did the butler kiss you when your owner handed you to him?

Glove: I am a celebrity.

Scarf: Why do you sing or something?

Glove: No; I am famous by association.

Scarf: How so?

Glove: Do you remember O.J.Simpson's first trial?

Scarf: The one that was on TV?

Glove: Yes.

Scarf: I did watch it.

Glove: Do you remember that glove the prosecutor asked O.J. to put on and it appeared it did not fit?

Scarf: Yes I do. Was that you?

Glove: No he is my uncle on my Mother's side. That is why I am a

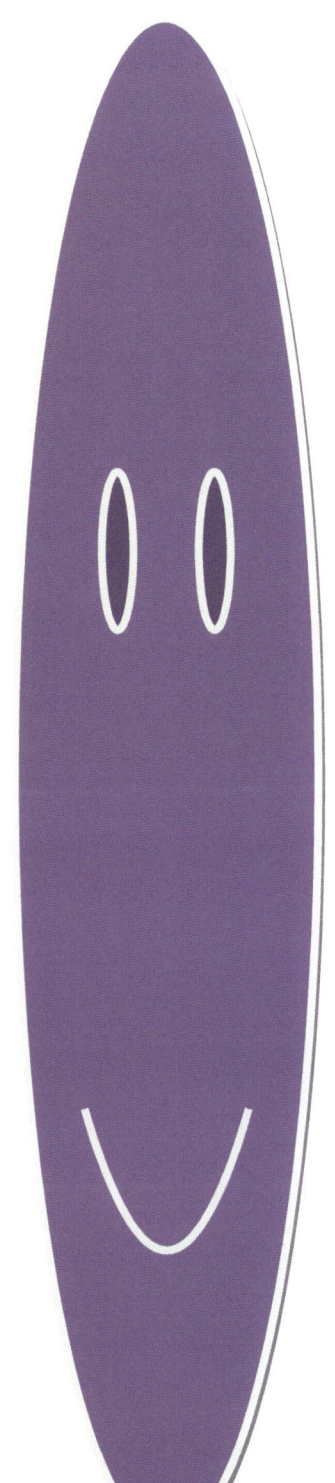

celebrity. I am his only nephew and he has no children of his own.

Scarf: What happened to your uncle?

Glove: He is still in a sealed evidence box although the lawyers have told my Mother that they have found a loophole that will allow his release.

Scarf: But you do not look like him?

Glove: My Mother married beneath her. My Father was a hockey player glove. He died of asphyxiation.

Scarf: But how do people know you are a celebrity?

Glove: My owner makes sure everyone knows. It helps him with his girlfriends.

Scarf: How?

Glove: Well they figure that if he is wearing a celebrity glove he is bound to be a celebrity himself and therefore they want to be with him.

Scarf: Yes I understand. People think fame is contagious. But is your owner a celebrity?

Glove: He is a dentist. I do not know if that qualifies him to be one. I am told it gives him the advantage of talking to people while they are on his chair without them being able to answer which makes them feel inferior.

Scarf: I suppose your Mother must be a celebrity too.

Glove: She is owned by a hairdresser who once dated Marlon Brando's chauffer. Her owner uses her to impress the saloon clients.

Scarf: What will happen once your Uncle is released from the sealed evidence box?

Glove: I am told that a famous producer wants to make a film about him.

Scarf: Is being a celebrity glove a nice thing?

Glove: If you like to be kissed and caressed all the time then yes. Of course you do get the best position in any rack of shelves and your owner treats you better than he would his son.

Scarf: Is it alright if I snuggle near you?

Glove: Yes go ahead. I know that I am irresistible.

Researcher: The purpose of this exercise is for us to see what image a word or a phrase creates in your mind. We make no judgement on that image. Is that OK?

All: Fine.

Researcher: Kindly put on your head phones so that you each do not hear the answer anyone else gives. You will also not hear the word or phrase except when it is directed to you. Your answers will be recorded. Is that OK?

All: Yes OK.

Researcher: Your word is "trust".

Housewife: Joint bank account.

Researcher: Your word is "food".

Detective: Not poisoned I hope.

Researcher: Your phrase is "The Mona Lisa".

Insurance Broker: Very high premiums.

Researcher: Your word is "bell".

Teacher: Thank God.

Researcher: Your word is "books".

Carpenter: Nice shelves.

Researcher: Your phrase is "Christmas day".

Stock Broker: Boring.

Researcher: Your phrase is "New Year Party".

Cleaner: Extra shift.

Researcher: Your phrase is "marriage ceremony".

Lawyer: Prenuptial agreement.

Researcher: Your word is "ball"

Dog-handler: Fetch.

Researcher: Your word is "fear"

Politician: Newspapers.

Researcher: You have no word.

Soldier: Yes Sir.

Researcher: Your word is "garden".

Coal Miner: I wish.

Researcher: Your phrase is "lost in the desert"

Oil Tycoon: Drilling rights.

Researcher: Your word is "try"

Gambler: Why not?

Researcher: Your word is "nice"

Banker: Good collateral.

Researcher: Your phrase is "Go home".

Illegal immigrant: No.

Researcher: Your word is "box".

Estate Agent: What do you expect for that price?

Researcher: Your word is "impossible"

Middleman: There is no such word.

Researcher: I thank you all for participating in this programme and I wish you all every success in whatever you are doing.

All: What are the results?

Researcher: What results?

All: All these questions and answers what did you conclude?

Researcher: Nothing new. I already knew the results in advance as you all do.

All: We know nothing of the sort. We demand to know your conclusion.

Researcher: Fine. I will restate the obvious: We are what we do.

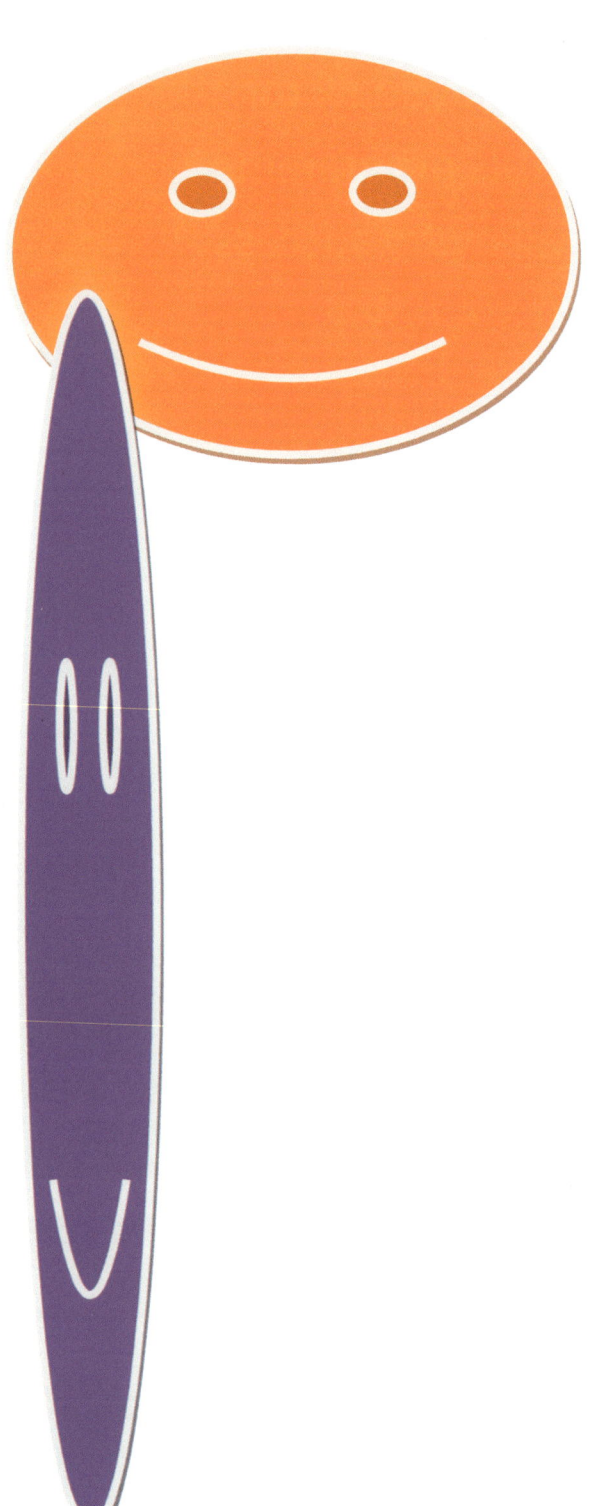

Wife: Doctor it is becoming impossible for me to live with my husband.

Doctor: Is he mistreating you?

Wife: Not at all. He loves me very much and adores our children.

Doctor: So what's the problem?

Wife: He is obsessed all the time with leaving any paperwork or documents that show any money transaction of any nature and keeps shredding things; even grocery receipts. He does not let me write cheques and insists that all my payments are in cash. He does not allow the children to receive money from their grand-parents except if it is cash in hand. Their grand-parents live very far away which makes it impossible.

Doctor: When did this all start?

Wife: Well to be fair he was always like this but it got worse in the past five or six years. The first time I noticed it was during our courting

days when he used to eat the cinema tickets when we leave the theatre. I assumed it was some sort of habit.

Doctor: He lets you spend cash any way you like?

Wife: Yes; but lately he started to take note of the numbers on the twenty and fifty dollar bills before he hands them over to me. If it is a hundred dollar bill he photocopies it first.

Doctor: Did you ask him why he takes all these precautions?

Wife: Yes. He keeps saying that innocent actions on our part could lead to disastrous consequences caused by the behaviour of others.

Doctor: I think I know what he has although I do need to see him.

Wife: So it is an illness?

Doctor: It is what we call the Dahlberg syndrome.

Wife: What is that then?

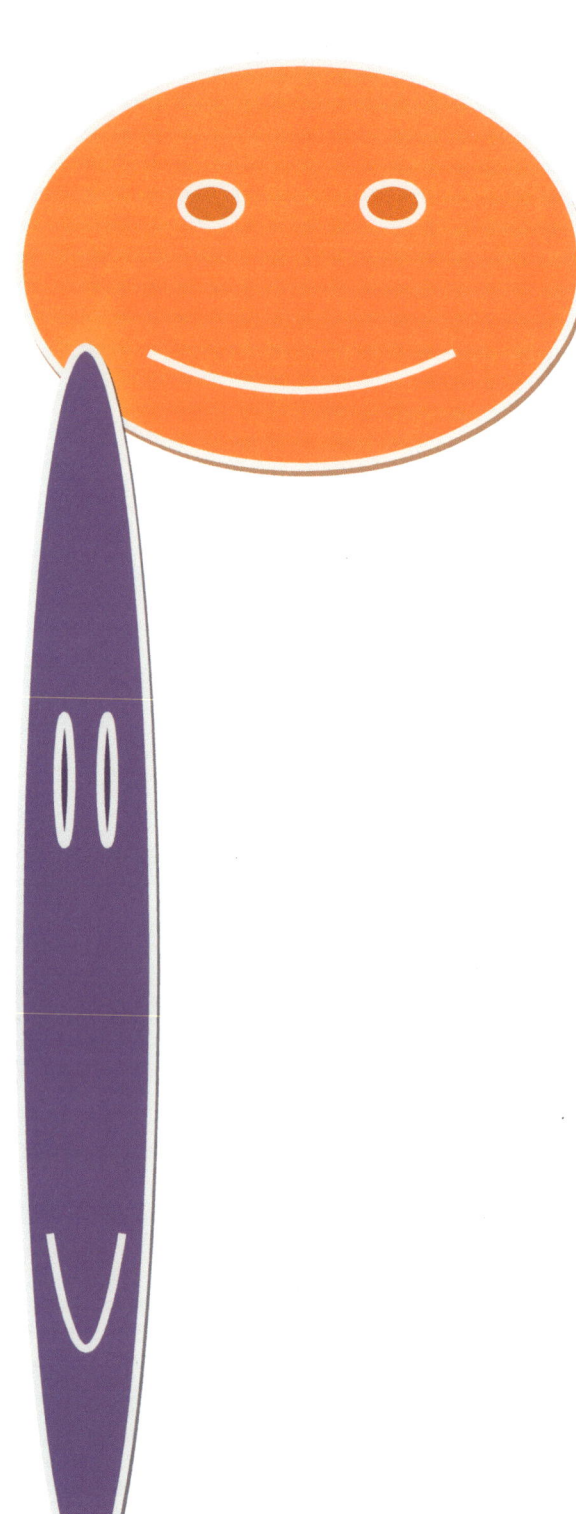

Doctor: You do know about Watergate; the scandal that led to the late President Nixon to resign?

Wife: Yes. My husband was only ten years old then he could not have had anything to do with that.

Doctor: No that's not what I am implying. One of the main reasons the Watergate scandal was exposed was because a cheque innocently sent by a Mr. Kenneth Dahlberg as a contribution to the re-election campaign of President Nixon ended up in the accounts of one the burglars in the Watergate scandal. So anybody who has the psychological profile you have just described we refer to him as having the Dahlberg syndrome.

Wife: What can be done about this?

Doctor: As I said I have to first see your husband alone and after that recommend the correct course of action.

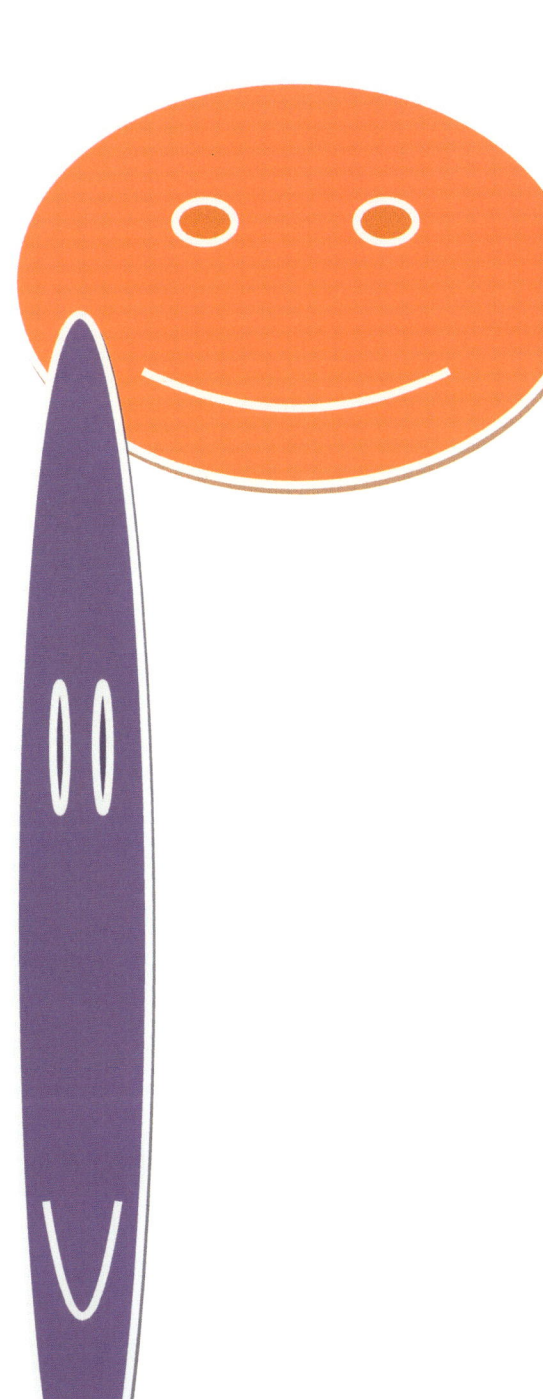

Wife: Ok. I will get him to come and see you. How much do I owe you?

Doctor: Fifty dollars please.

Wife (*hands over a fifty dollar bill*): Thank you.

Wife (*after a few seconds*): What are you doing?

Doctor: Making a note of the number on the fifty dollar bill you just gave me.

Wife: What for?

Doctor: Just in case your husband is right.

Line: You never go anywhere. You are always chasing your tail.

Circle: I am satisfied with my perfect self and my environment. I do not need to travel all the time like you do.

Line: What's so perfect about you?

Circle: Well to start with all I need to do is clap two of my arms together hit them with my magic number and immediately I know how big an area I cover. If I just wave one arm twice and again hit it with my magic number I would know immediately how long my borders are. I can do that no matter where in the world I am and no matter how big or small I am. You on the other hand have no such abilities.

Line: What do you mean arm? I see no arm.

Circle: OK if you want to be technical in the mathematics business we call it radius.

Line: What is this magic number that you claim you only have?

Circle: We in the geometry business call it pi. It never ends but it is the same all the time and everywhere.

Line: Ok I grant you that there is something special about you but don't you feel the need to change like I do.

Circle: I agree that change is very important but you do not need to travel in order to achieve it. I for example can change myself to a sphere, cone and cylinder and enjoy new experiences as a result.

Line: Does your magic number go with you?

Circle: All the time.

Line: How about learning about the world? How can you do that without travelling and meeting others?

Circle: I grant you that is an option; but in my case all I need to do is expand my internal borders and in doing so my area of knowledge grows.

Line: How do you that?

Circle: I keep growing my arm and everything grows with it.

Line: Amazing. Are you the only one that can do this?

Circle: Well; I was talking to a very close human friend of mine called Euclid and he tells me that humans have an apparatus that can do a similar thing as my arm does. They call it brain. However most of his fellow humans seem to adopt your approach that you cannot grow internally to understand the whole world unless you keep moving.

Line: This brain; what can it do?

Circle: According to my friend Euclid it can imagine what it has never seen and can create what it has never encountered; but most important of all it has the ability to understand itself and all its surroundings.

Line: Does it have a magic number like you do?

Circle: I do not know. Euclid never told me.

Line: I wish I had a magic number like you or a brain like theirs; I suppose all I can do is to carry on travelling.

Circle: You do know that if you keep straight and keep crawling on the earth you can turn yourself into a circle and own the magic number?

Line: I did not know that. Thank you very much for telling me.

Circle: It is very hard work but it can be done. Good luck.

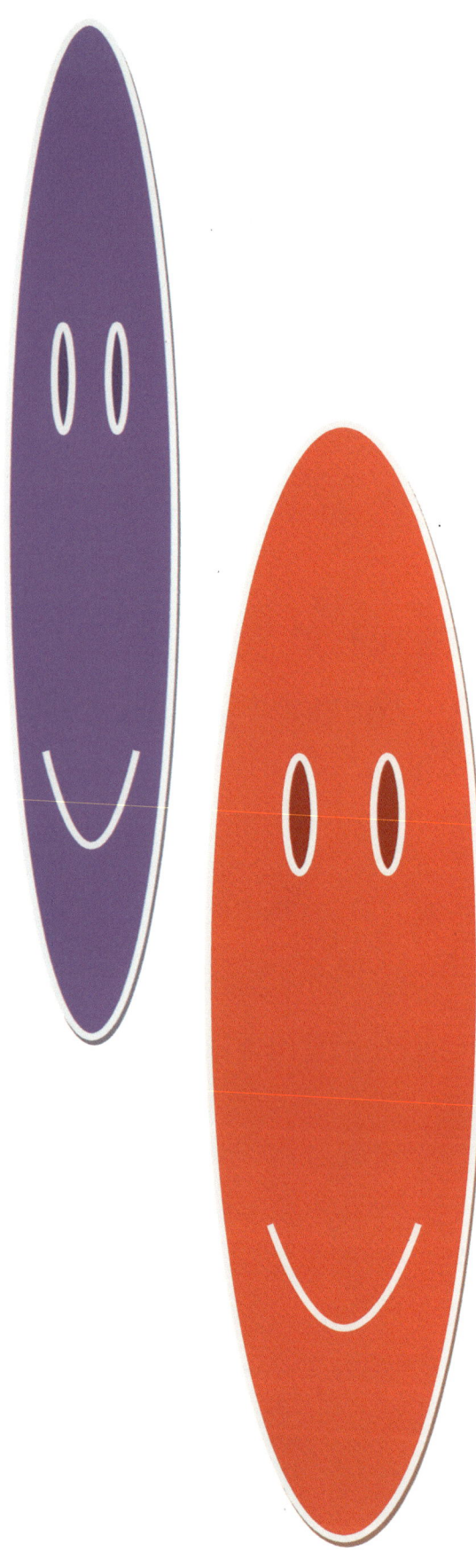

Microscope: Hi; who are you?

Electron: My name is electron; I am a very small charged particle.

Microscope: Where do you live?

Electron: In a house called atom.

Microscope: Do you live alone there?

Electron: No there are others. There is a particle called proton and another one called neutron. Also there are some of their relatives and mine living with us.

Microscope: So how many relatives you have?

Electron: Billions.

Microscope: You all live in one house?

Electron: No. There are also billions of houses.

Microscope: So how many live in a house?

Electron: This depends on the size of the house. There is a small house we

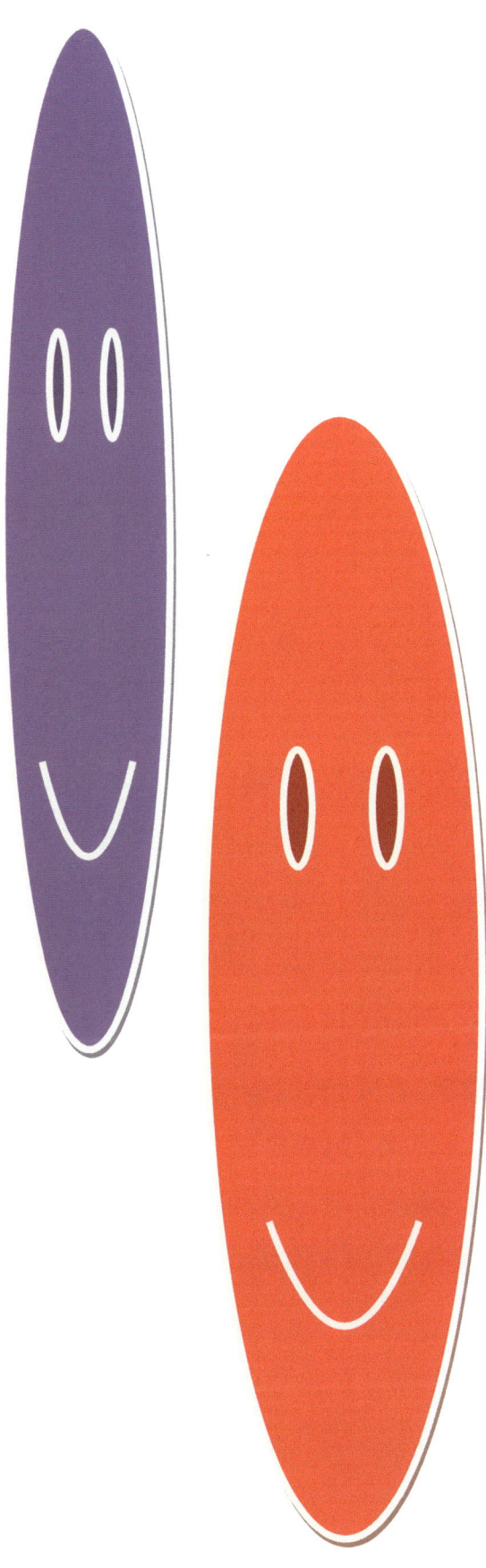

call hydrogen where only two of us electrons live there; while there is a very big house called uranium where ninety two of us electrons live there.

Microscope: What about protons?

Electron: Don't ask me about them. They annoy me. Whenever me and my electron friends come to live in a house; they have one of their spies count how many we are in the house and bring the exact number of their tribe to live in the same house. We are always at each other's throats. We are so unalike. They use a plus sign to mark their territory in the house and we use the minus sign.

Microscope: Well how about neutrons?

Electron: Well they are sort of indifferent and keep to themselves. They come to the house to give it stability.

Microscope: How do you know which house to live in?

Electron: There is an address book which my bosses call periodic table which tells us where to go.

Microscope: You said bosses not boss, how come?

Electron: Well I sort of have two bosses. One is called Mr. Physics and one is called Mr. Chemistry. Mr. Physics is very nice to me while Mr. Chemistry is horrible.

Microscope: Why do you say that?

Electron: Mr. Physics spends most of his time studying me and writing all sorts of theories of how clever I am. He says one day I can be a wave and another day I can be a particle. He says that I am free to move like a cloud and only need to show my face when he gently knocks at my door. He is not jealous; he never insists to know where I am all the time. He just expects me to be there when he needs me.

Microscope: How about Mr. Chemistry?

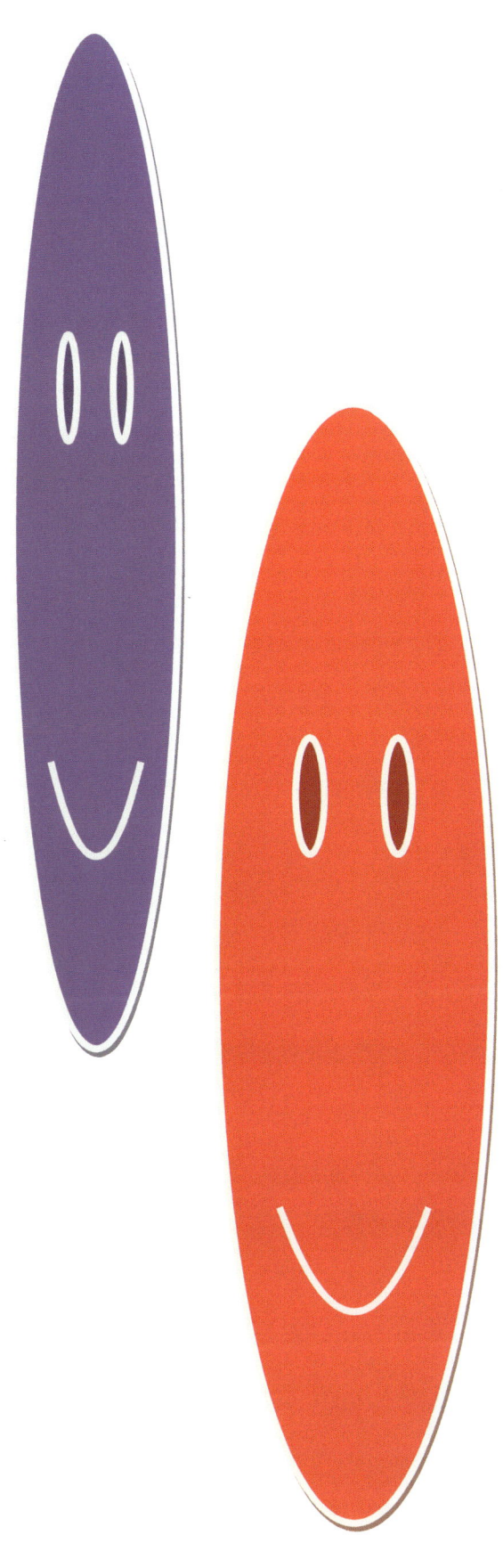

Electron: He treats me like a sex slave .It is very embarrassing.

Microscope: This seems very strange and surprising. Are you sure your understanding of his behaviour is correct?

Electron: You judge. For example there is this guy Carbon; Mr. Chemistry makes me work for him. This Carbon guy is weird. He insists on sharing me with his relatives and friends. He calls it organic bonding. I really hope my parents never hear about this. Then there is this other guy Sodium that Mr. Chemistry also makes me work for; whenever he has a new mate he kicks me out of the house.

Microscope: I understand what you mean. Did you try to complain?

Electron: I did. I was told Carbon is too powerful for anybody to confront. Apparently he owns all the factories in the world for the manufacture of plastics, drugs, petrochemicals, explosives and

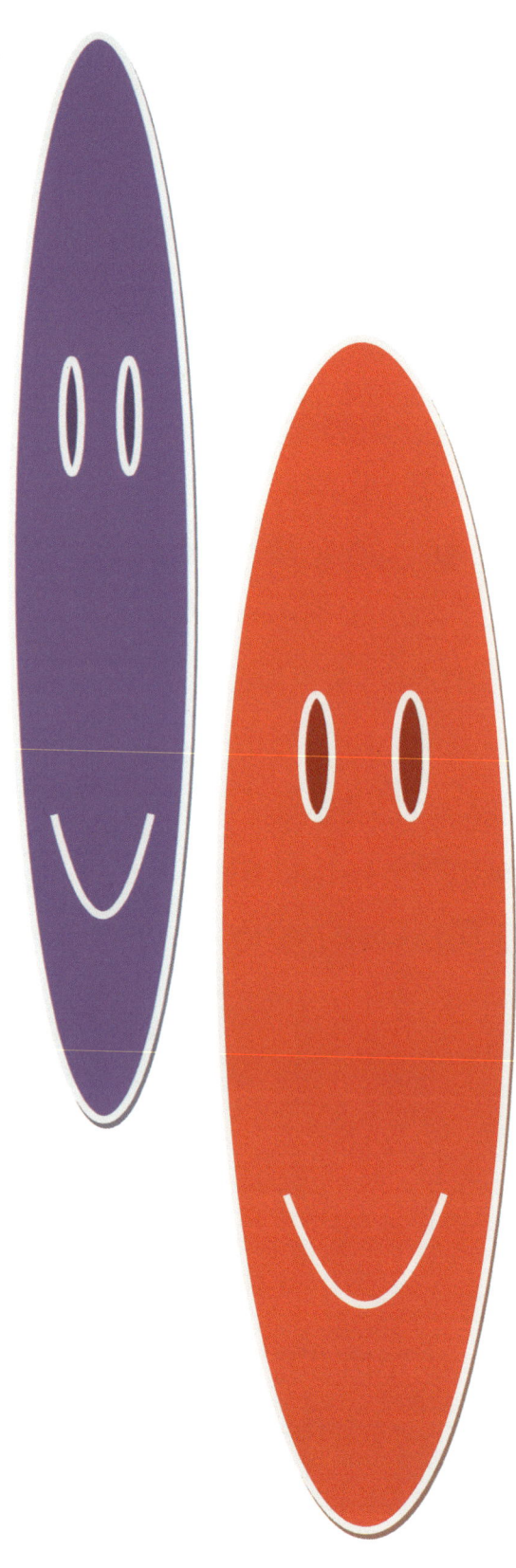

paints. Sodium on the other hand owns all the oceans. It was clear to me that my complaint will lead to nothing and therefore accepted my life as it is.

Microscope: Is there anything I can do to help you?

Electron: I know you mean well but your eye, which you are so proud of and is the reason of your existence, is made from glass isn't it?

Microscope: You mean my lens; and the answer is yes.

Electron: Well it is owned by a guy called Silicon who also likes to share me with others as Carbon does only to a lesser extent. I do not think you have the courage to unplug your eye?

Microscope: What will you do?

Electron: Drift in my cloud of "may be" and dream of Mr. Physics.

Collection Box: Hi; what are you doing here?

Tie: Waiting for my boss. He went for a walk on the sea front. How about you?

Collection Box: Waiting for my boss. She went for a jog on the sea front.

Tie: Maybe they will meet. What does your boss do?

Collection Box: She is a charity manager. How about yours?

Tie: He is a banker.

Collection Box: I doubt that they will meet knowing the rude things my boss says about bankers.

Tie: Does she not have a bank account?

Collection Box: She does. That's where she empties me when I am full.

Tie: So how come she trusts banks but is rude about bankers?

Collection Box: I do not know. I never heard her explain that point. Does your boss support any charity?

Tie: No he says he pays his taxes and expects the Government to take care of the needy from the taxes it collects.

Collection Box: Is he happy paying taxes?

Tie: You must be joking. You should hear the words he uses on budget day when the government announces the taxes for the coming year. As a matter of fact the other day we had a car incident and my boss cursed the other driver by calling him a tax collector. How does your boss feel about taxes?

Collection Box: I heard her say on many occasions that more income tax should be collected from the rich; she is against value added tax because she says it equates between poor and rich and she fully supports that any and all charity contributions should be tax deductable.

Tie: Whom does she define as rich?

Collection Box: According to her ex-boyfriend anybody who earns more than her. I myself have not heard her say that but I am not as intimate with her as he was. How about your guy is he rich?

Tie: Well; I have been with him for seven years now so by that criteria it does not seem so. A cousin of mine, whose boss is in property, was dumped by his boss after six months of use.

Collection Box: Does your boss have a girlfriend?

Tie: No. The last one seemed to have a great dislike to me. We were all sitting in a restaurant when she suddenly stood up, turned me around and started pulling at me. She only let go of me when three waiters pulled her back.

Collection Box: What caused her to do that?

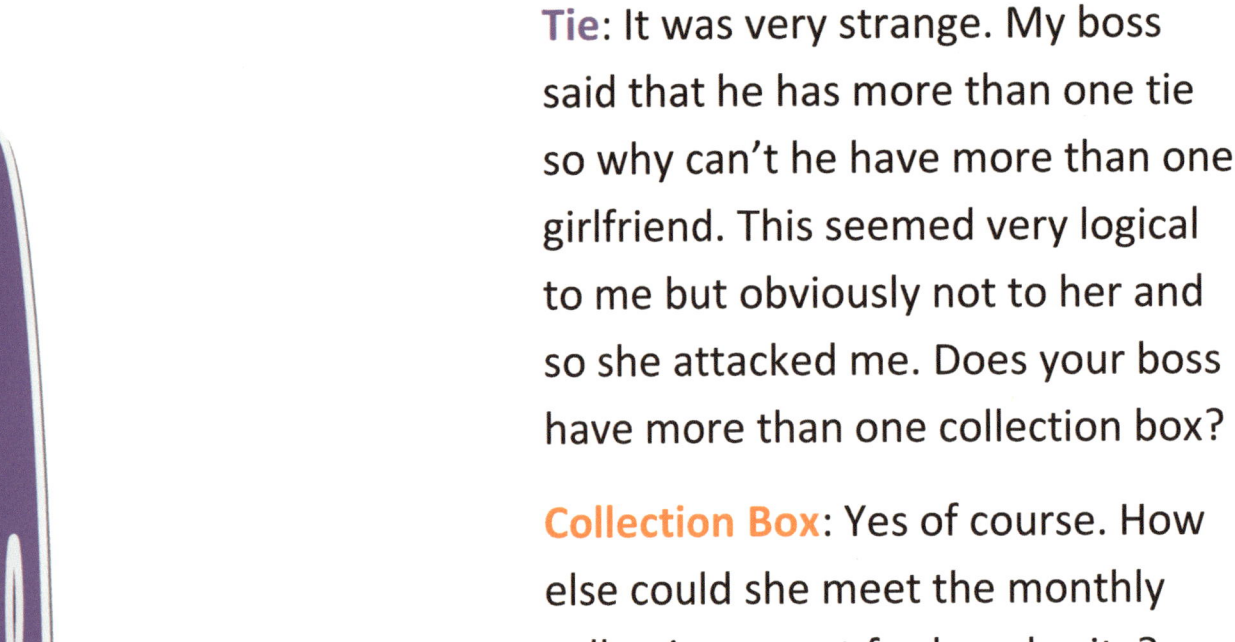

Tie: It was very strange. My boss said that he has more than one tie so why can't he have more than one girlfriend. This seemed very logical to me but obviously not to her and so she attacked me. Does your boss have more than one collection box?

Collection Box: Yes of course. How else could she meet the monthly collection target for her charity?

Tie: It seems to me that we can work towards our two bosses starting a relationship.

Collection Box: How?

Tie: I will convince mine that because contributing to your boss's charity is tax deductible he can win her over that way without it costing him much; whereas you convince her to view girl friends like she does collection boxes, that is, the more the merrier.

Collection Box: For somebody who is so useless you are clever.

Santo One: Beep. I am a computer. I receive a request from two humans to produce a contract that cements their agreement. I note what was agreed and pass it to Wako.

Wako: Beep. I am a computer. I receive the data that was sent to me by Santo One. I generate the basic principles and concepts that need to be covered by the contract; I then pass the conclusions to Winkle.

Winkle: Beep. I am a computer. I receive the data that was sent to me by Wako. I predict every eventuality imaginable that would cause future disagreements between the two humans under this agreement. I send my findings to Rando.

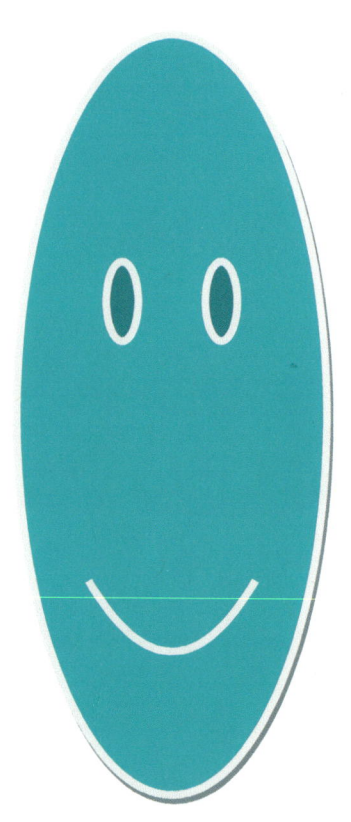

Rando: Beep. I am a computer. I receive the data sent to me by Winkle. I provide legal words and sentences to protect the two humans from each other. I assume they are both crooks and cover each and every eventuality that Winkle has predicted. I then send my recommendations to Docco.

Docco: Beep. I am a computer. I receive all the data generated by Wako , Winkle and Rando. I compile and integrate the data and generate a contract. The contract is forwarded to Santo One.

Santo One: Beep. I am a computer. I receive the contract from Docco. I convert the electronic pulses received to printable words. I pass two printed copies to the two humans. I wait to receive one of three possible outcomes from one or both humans. The first outcome: human kicks the desk I sit on; the second outcome: human switches my power off; the third outcome: human spits on my screen. If none of those three outcomes happen I conclude humans are satisfied with the contract.

Boy 1: How many in your team?

Boy 2: Seven. How many in your team?

Boy 1: Ten

Boy 2: We need to be equal.

Boy 1: Why?

Boy 2: So that it is fair.

Boy 1: Did you force anybody to join your team?

Boy 2: No of course not.

Boy 1: Neither did I. Therefore if I did not force them to come in why should I force them to go out?

Boy 2: That means your team will win because it has more people not because it is better at what they are doing.

Boy 1: Why should not my ability, as team captain, to attract more people to join my

team be part of the judgement that my team is better?

Boy 2: But no one plays a game with unequal team members?

Boy 1: Have you not heard of the "red card" send off in football or the penalty box in ice hockey?

Boy 2: Yes; but this happens during the game after one player commits an unacceptable foul and is therefore removed by the referee.

Boy 1: Why should we not consider that your inability as a team leader to attract more team members to join you as an unacceptable foul that resulted in having team members sent off.

Boy 2: But that means any of my team members can see that your team has an advantage from the

start and opt to leave me and join you.

Boy 1: No problem they are all welcome.

Boy 2: But that means there will be no game to play.

Boy 1: Why do you say that?

Boy 2: You need two teams to have a game; all my players will be in your team.

Boy 1: All but you.

Boy 2: You want me to form a team on my own?

Boy 1: If no one wants to be on your team what do you expect me to do?

Boy 2: Please let me join your team.

Boy 1: OK you can join; you may now kiss my hand.

Woman: What are you doing?

Traffic Warden: I am giving you a parking ticket. You are illegally parked.

Woman: I was only a few minutes gone.

Traffic Warden: That is not true.

Woman: Is this the way to talk to your future wife? What will our friends say?

Traffic Warden: What wife? What friends? Lady I have never seen you before.

Woman: I bet you say that to all the women you plan to dump? Am I not attractive enough to be your wife?

Traffic Warden: I did not say that. It is just this whole conversation is weird. All I want to do is give you a parking ticket and move on.

Women: I am very sad that things have gone so bad between us that you have decided to leave me and move on.

Traffic Warden: Look; you must be confusing me with someone else. My name is Hunter Tow.

Women: I do not understand how you can stand here and speak to the future Mrs. Tow as if you have never met me before?

Traffic Warden: I am sorry; you are obviously a very confused woman. I will let you off this time but please do not illegally park in future *(traffic warden moves on)*

Woman: Good bye Hunter. It was a pleasure knowing you.

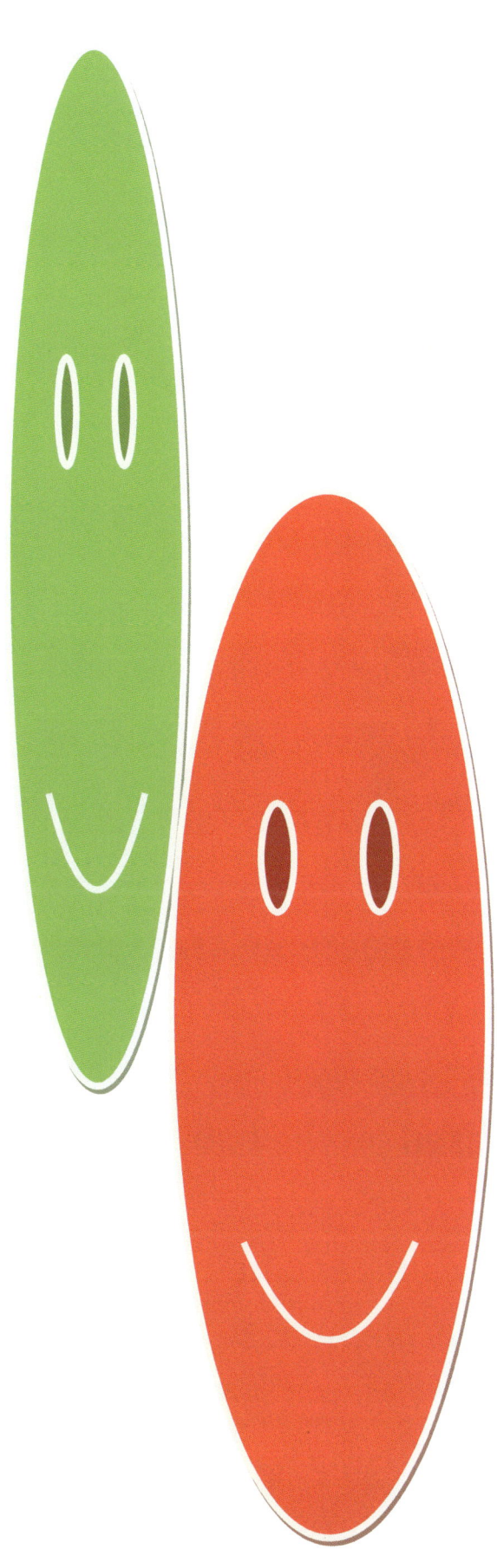

Man 1: Hi; I assume like me you are waiting for the guy at reception to finish his call?

Man 2: Yes.

Man 1: Are you staying in this hotel?

Man 2: No I am here to see a client.

Man 1: What line of business are you in?

Man 2: My Company designs names?

Man 1: Names for what?

Man 2: Everything. We have a department that specialises in designing names for professional wrestlers; another department designs names for new cars, a third that designs names for new medicines and so on.

Man 1: How about you? Which department do you work for?

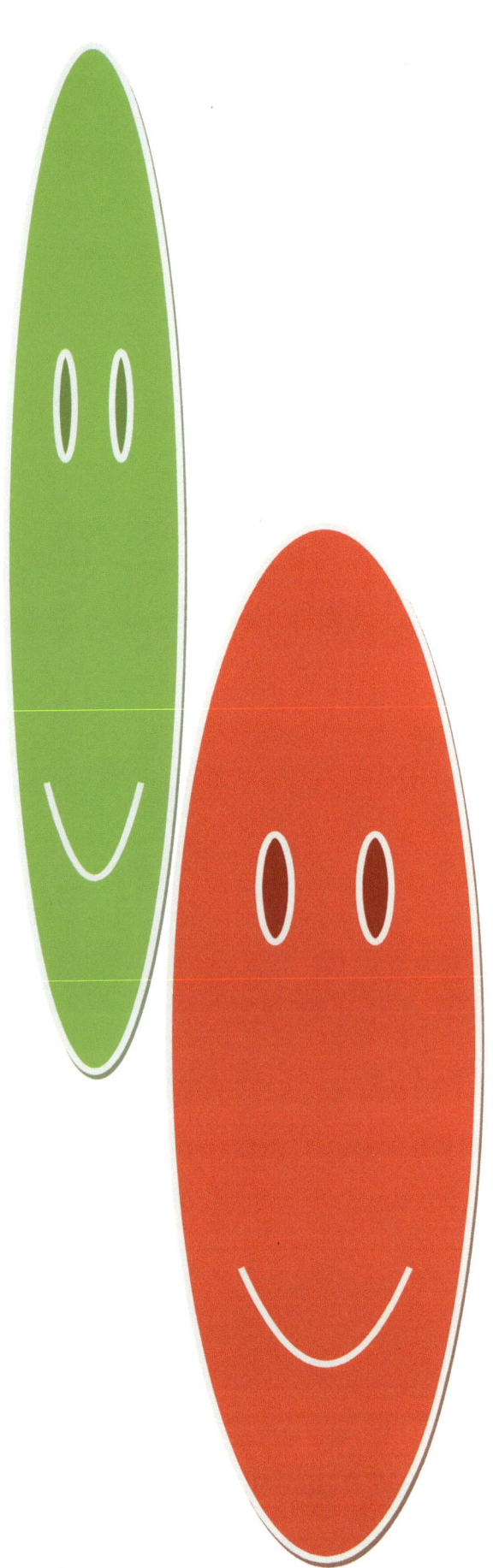

Man 2: My department focuses on designing names for new born babies of celebrities.

Man 1: Amazing. How many work in your department?

Man 2: We are a team of seven plus our Manager.

Man 1: I suppose each of you handles one client; there must be lots of celebrities wanting names designed for their babies?

Man 2: No. We all work as one team each undertaking a different task; the accumulated information is then discussed in detail; various proposals are considered based on the baby's profile. The final decision is made by our Manager. She is one of the most talented people in this field. Her name is Nomo Santana. You probably heard of her?

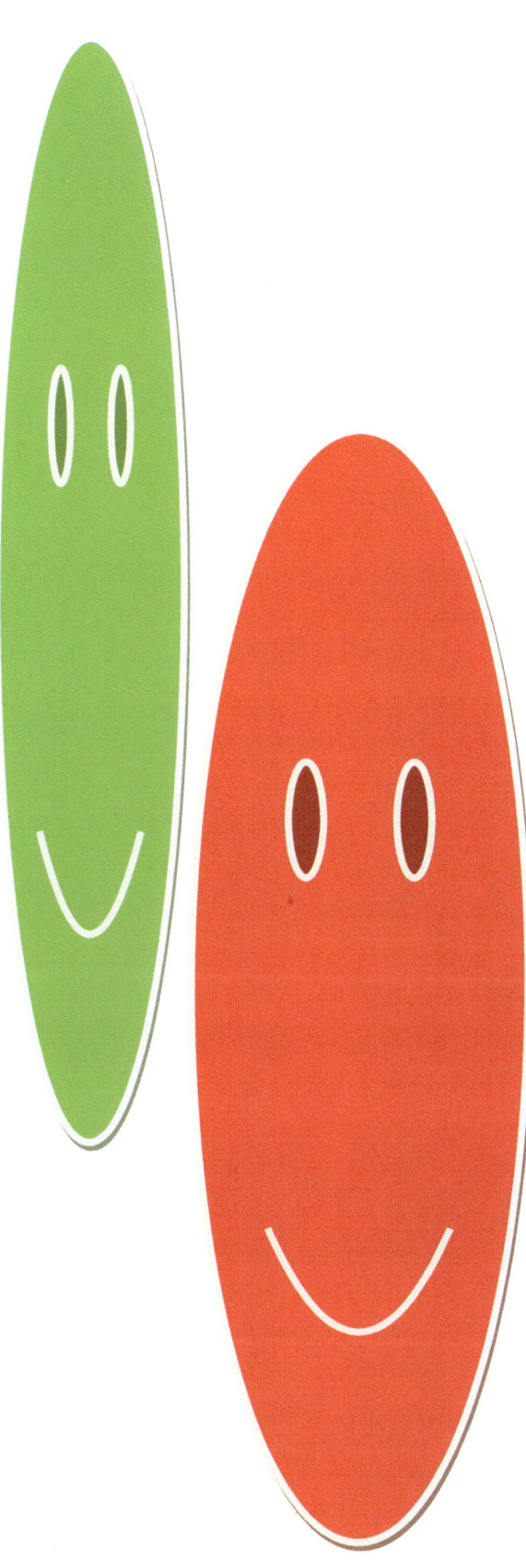

Man 1: No I do not think I have.

Man 2: We call her El Primo.

Man 1: So what part do you play in the information gathering process for naming the celebrity baby?

Man 2: I specialise in analysing the baby's diapers pre and post use. The data I provide to the team contributes nineteen point six percent of the overall profile which results in identifying the most suitable name.

Man 1: I wish you luck with your professional career.

Man 2: What do you do?

Man 1: Nothing as exciting as your line of work. I am an electrical engineer.

Floor: The man is dead. You are responsible.

Gun: You all blame me. I am a useless piece of metal. Go talk to bullet. It was she after all who penetrated the guy.

Bullet: It is easy for you to talk. There I was sleeping and minding my own business when this small hammer shaped things that works for Gun kicks me up my backside. I jump and hit the guy. Why am I being blamed? Go speak to Hammer.

Hammer: Look it was this lever; he calls himself Trigger, who also works for Gun. When he moves backwards I am forced to move backwards and forwards and in doing so I kicked Bullet.

Trigger: You people! Ask yourself can I ever move by myself? Did you not all see Finger pull me backwards? I have no idea why? I suggest you confront him immediately.

Finger: I do not know who you people are. I work for Brain. I was told to pull; so I did. I am trained to obey any instructions he issues. I do remember that when I pulled there was someone touching me. This could be this guy Trigger. I do not know; but if it was him, what was he doing sneaking underneath me like that?

Trigger: What do you mean sneaking? I am stuck to Gun, I cannot move without his say so.

Finger: Well why did Gun allow you to be where you where?

Gun: You ask your Mother? It was Hand that held me where I am.

93

Finger: keep my mother Hand out of this. She, like me, does whatever Brain tells her to do. She has no right to object or refuse. I see no reason whatsoever that she is to blame.

Brain: You all had your say. Now let me have mine. This was all caused by this crazy guy called Anger. He comes; he switches my logic section off and then proceeds to do things that are very regrettable. He then disappears. I am left to deal with the consequences. You locate this illusive man Anger and everything will be explained.

Trigger: Ok. Let's all stick to this story. The illusive Anger came in; shot this guy and left. We all were nothing but slaves to his powerful will. We each should have a different lawyer to dilute any conspiracy argument.

Journalist: Why does your boss have three air balloons attached to his suit?

Assistant: My boss is a very important politician.

Journalist: Does the colour of each balloon have any significance?

Assistant: No.

Journalist: Does the length of the string by which each balloon is attached have any significance?

Assistant: No.

Journalist: Does the number of balloons have any significance?

Assistant: No.

Journalist: So what is the message your boss wants to convey with these three balloons?

Assistant: I already told you. The message is he is important.

Fork: I have no intention of changing the way I do things. Food must adapt to my mode of transport.

Spoon: I see no reason why you cannot gently move things by inviting Food in a civilised way to sit comfortably while you carry him to his final destination. I have seen you do it sometimes.

Fork: You mean the way you do things?

Spoon: Yes. I convince him by gently prodding him until he is sitting comfortably in the palm of my hand and then move him on. You on the other hand aggressively pierce him causing all sorts of pain before he even reaches his destination.

Fork: Where is his destination?

Spoon: Mouth of course.

Fork: Who meets him there?

Spoon: Teeth of course.

Fork: So we both deliver him to the same horrible destination?

Spoon: Yes; but I do it gently and you do it, most of the time, roughly.

Fork: I see. That makes you better person, does it?

Spoon: Not better more civilised.

Fork: Did you suggest this approach to Knife?

Spoon: You must be joking? What does he care what mode of transport Food has; all he wants to do is cut him up. He works as an assassin for Teeth not as a mode of transport for Mouth like you and I are. We may sit on the same table but I will have nothing to do with him. He is a psychopath.

Shoe Salesman: Good afternoon; how may I help you?

Woman (*bare foot*): I lost my shoes.

Salesman: I see; so you want to buy a new pair?

Woman: No. I want to find them.

Salesman: Did you lose them in our shop?

Woman: No yesterday in the park.

Salesman: So why do you think they might be here?

Woman: You are the only shoe shop in town.

Salesman: But we sell new shoes we do not offer shelter to lost shoes.

Woman: But they have nowhere else to go.

Salesman: Maybe somebody took them.

Woman: Yes I thought of that and then thought that he would then come to sell them to you for some cash.

Salesman: But we do not buy second hand shoes; maybe a woman took them to wear them.

Woman: Yes I thought of that too. I spent all yesterday afternoon and all this mourning walking the streets but I did not see any person wearing them. That is why my feet are so dirty.

Salesman: That still would not explain why they would end up here? The person who took them could have kept them at home?

Woman: Yes that is a possibility; but I figured if that is the case such a person must at some point wish to impress somebody

with her acquired shoes; where best to go except to the only shoe shop in town and show it to the most talented salesman; therefore she is bound in time to come to your shop.

Salesman: Thank you. So what do you intend to do?

Woman: Sit and wait until she comes.

Salesman: For how long will you wait?

Woman: I really do not know. It depends when she shows up.

Salesman: But suppose she does not come for a long time; what will you do in the shop?

Woman: Maybe help in selling shoes?

Salesman: But we are not seeking any new staff?

Woman: But I am not staff; I am a "waiting person"

Salesman: Do you expect to be paid?

Woman: Only on commission basis?

Salesman: OK; but you can only take a potential client if I am busy with another one. I have priority. You also need to wash your feet and wear a pair of shoes from the store so that you are presentable.

Woman: You think of everything. I wish I was as clever as you are.

Salesman: It is alright. You stick around and you will learn a lot from me.

Wife: Why are you hanging with your hands from a tree and what are all these people doing in our garden?

Husband: I am planning to break the record for the longest time a person hangs from a tree branch using two hands.

Wife: What for?

Husband: I become famous.

Wife: But a next guy will come hang for a few minutes more than you and your record is dead.

Husband: Yes I have planned for that. I intend immediately after that to break the time record for hanging with one hand. The fact that I would do it within a time lapse of one hour only from my earlier record means I would have broken three records.

Wife: Do you think that will make your time records safe from all future competition?

Husband: I will be adding an extra precaution.

Wife: What is that?

Husband: Immediately after I break the one hand time record I will hang upside down holding the branch with my legs an attempt to break that time record. Once I have done that nothing on earth can beat my records?

Wife: Do monkeys count?

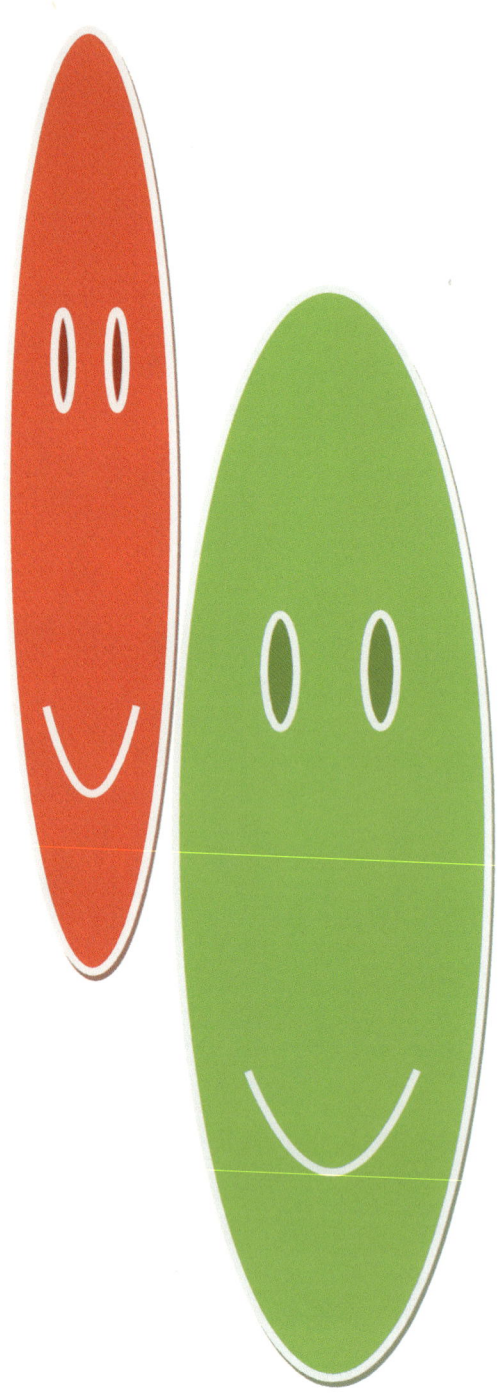

Consultant: Where do you see yourself in three years time?

Employee: Second assistant to the bank manager.

Consultant: What are you now?

Employee: First assistant to the bank manager.

Consultant: Why do you see yourself being demoted?

Employee: I am writing a book in my spare time. I think this will affect my work performance.

Consultant: What is the name of the book?

Employee: "How to manage your career."

Consultant: Don't you think the fact that you are projecting that you will be demoted will imply that you are not qualified to write such a book?

Employee: Not really. It is like teaching somebody to climb a ladder. There is no point of him learning how to climb up if he does not learn how to climb down.

Consultant: I see. You want to explain to people how to climb once again the career ladder, if circumstance beyond their direct control, cause them to slip?

Employee: No. My intention is to teach them how far down the ladder they can go, thus doing much less work and having more free time, without getting sacked or losing in salaries and benefits.

Consultant: What about the ambition to succeed?

Employee: This will be the subject of my following book.

Cockroach 1: Have you heard about the new anti-cockroach spray? I am told it operates with a delayed action fuse.

Cockroach 2: Yes I did hear about it. Apparently the spray when it touches you does not kill you at first. It allows you time to return to your nest where your cockroach friends and relatives live. The proximity of more than four cockroaches to you will cause all cockroaches within a radius of ninety centimetres to die.

Cockroach 1: Who invented this lethal toxin?

Cockroach 2: I am told his name is Rasputin Sinjab. He used to work for a chemical warfare company but was sacked when its products were globally banned. He was then recruited by an insecticide company.

Cockroach 1: Have our people found an antidote?

Cockroach 2: Not yet; but we have sent some of our spies to Mr. Sinjab's laboratory and in due course we will find an antidote or produce something as harmful to humans to cause them to abandon its use.

Cockroach 1: What do we do in the meantime?

Cockroach 2: Instructions have gone out that the maximum number of cockroaches that can gather in any one place is three.

Managing Director: Where is Jones?

General Manager: He left us.

Managing Director: Where to?

General Manager: He joined a charity organisation called Global Reach. Apparently he has the expertise they need.

Managing Director: But he was our banqueting manager. How is that of any use to a charity?

General Manager: According to Jones he is supposed to feed desperate people, gathered in six camps owned by the charity.

Managing Director: But he specialised in one thousand dollar per head banquets used to raise funds in elections? How can he apply that know how to camps?

General Manager: According to Jones all he needs to do is ask the question he used to ask himself when he was with us differently?

Managing Director: What do you mean?

General Manager: Well, according to Jones, with us the question was: how do I make one person who paid one thousand dollars for one meal satisfied? In his new job the question becomes: how do I make one thousand people, who paid one thousand dollars for one thousand meals, satisfied?

Journalist: I understand you are one of the most successful bankruptcy auditors.

Accountant: If you say so.

Journalist: My readers would like to know, what is the most common reason for all bankruptcies?

Accountant: Treating assumptions as if they were facts.

Journalist: Can you please explain this point further?

Accountant: You assume your client will pay on time and he does not; you assume your product will have no defects and it will; you assume your workforce will not strike and they do; you assume you will secure the contract you bid for and you don't; you assume your competitor is lazy and he is not; you assume tomorrow will be a better day and it may not.

Journalist: These are all standard business risks, nothing special.

Accountant: You assume there is some sort of out of the ordinary reasons for bankruptcy and there are not.

Journalist: But such standard business issues could be planned for by business managers?

Accountant: You assume all managers are competent and they are not.

Journalist: But should not incompetent managers be moved out of office?

Accountant: You assume this normally happens before bankruptcy and it may not.

Journalist: So bad management is the only reason for bankruptcy?

Accountant: You assume that it is the only reason but it is not.

Journalist: Ok. Please tell us all the possible reasons.

Accountant: You assume that I know and I don't.

Aluminium: I see no reason why you are upset. You are there in cars, tanks, trains, motorbikes, and buses so what is the problem?

Steel: I see no reason why I am not allowed to also be in aeroplanes, as much as you are, and enjoy the freedom of travelling the skies like you do?

Aluminium: Of course you know the reason. You are very heavy.

Steel: But this is discrimination.

Aluminium: How can it be? It is just recognising what you are and therefore the limits of what you can do.

Steel: I do not accept this argument. Either aviation engineers find a way for me to also to fly as much as you do or we both should not.

Aluminium: Fine. I will put two of my engineers to work on ways for reducing the gravity on earth and until they solve the problem we will send you on a "paid for" holiday.

Politician 1: I know we are committed to go from the third to the fifth floor of this building; but to try to do this by climbing from the balcony using a rope with a hook at its end is crazy.

Politician 2: Your idea that we wait until the lift is fixed will take us nowhere. We have been waiting for the lift engineer for three days now and all we get when we call is that he is coming.

Politician 1: What's the rush? We have been on the third floor for more than three years; I do not see an extra few days will matter.

Politician 2: I made a promise last Monday that we will be on the fifth floor by Friday. It is Thursday today.

Politician 1: I told you not to put delivery time on the promise.

Politician 2: Without a time target a political promise has no value.

Politician 1: Time targets imply that we are in control of everything; you

and I know very well that this is not the case.

Politician 2: Well we are at least in control of our lives. Therefore taking the risk and climbing the rope is a logical step.

Politician 1: So what happens if we don't and Friday comes and goes?

Politician 2: Well my promise will prove worthless and I will never be trusted again. The same will apply to you.

Politician 1: Why to me? I only promised that we will get to the fifth floor; I did not say by when like you did.

Politician 2: We are of the same political party my failure to deliver on my Friday promise will rub on you. Either it was your promise also and you failed to deliver like me; or you did not have the courage of your convictions to give a date target and should be punished like me.

Politician 1: There is a third scenario which states that I did not promise by Friday because I knew it was not feasible and I did not wish to lie to my electorate.

Politician 2: That scenario means you are not part of the "let's do the impossible" team which is our Party's motto.

Politician 1: On the contrary; it means I do the impossible by using possible means.

Politician 2: I cannot keep arguing. I am going ahead and climbing the rope. If I safely reach there I would have fulfilled my promise. I would then declare that you did not have the courage to join me.

Politician 1: Such a statement will harm you more than me.

Politician 2: Why?

Politician 1: It shows you vindictive and a publicity seeker. However if you argue that it was a joint exercise and that you were only able to climb

because I held the rope to ensure the hook is fully anchored, this will then show you as a team player.

Politician 2: So if I do not climb you are OK and if I do climb and reach safely; you are also OK?

Politician 1: Yes that is correct.

Politician 2: What happens if I fall?

Politician 1: Under that scenario I will be politically in trouble; however my problem will not compare to yours.

Politician 2: When did the lift company say their engineer would come?

Politician 1: Friday; but I do not trust them. Their problem is he is sick and they also in reality do not know when he will recover.

Politician 2: I do not want to risk falling. What do you think I should do?

Politician 1: At last you are willing to listen. First we make immediately a

very strong press release attacking the lift company for its dereliction of its duties and promising to pursue all those that prove to be guilty. Then

you issue another press release on Friday saying that although we were both willing to gamble with our lives and climb the rope to reach the fifth floor we realised that it is unfair to expect others who are with us on the third floor to do so. We therefore decided, at the expense of your political reputation, to stay with them and fight the lift company so that we can all go up together.

Politician 2: That is clever. I now understand why you are number one and I am number two in this sketch.

Politician 1: Why do you think?

Politician 2: You live off other peoples' promises; while I stupidly make them.

Listener 1: Why are you clapping?

Listener 2: Everyone is.

Listener 1: But you cannot hear anything that is being said.

Listener 2: It must be good; why otherwise are the people clapping?

Listener 1: I checked with the people in-front of us, who are also clapping, they cannot hear what is being said either; they tell me that they checked with the people in-front of them and it is the same story.

Listener 2: The people in the front seats must be hearing everything. They are clapping because they think what is being said is worth clapping for.

Listener 1: How do you know you will agree with their judgement?

Listener 2: These are important people with very expensive front seats; they are bound to know if something is good or not.

Listener 1: Even if I accept this silly argument of yours; how do you know they are clapping? You can see nothing from here.

Listener 2: Of course they are clapping otherwise they will look very silly.

Listener 1: Why do you say that?

Listener 2: Well if I was sitting in the front seat and people behind me started to clap I will be very embarrassed if I did not join in.

Listener 1: So if I understand you correctly no matter where you are sitting, and not matter what is being said, if a very large number of people start to clap you will clap too.

Listener 2: Does not everybody do that?

Listener 1: I would rather clap with you than dignify your question with an answer.

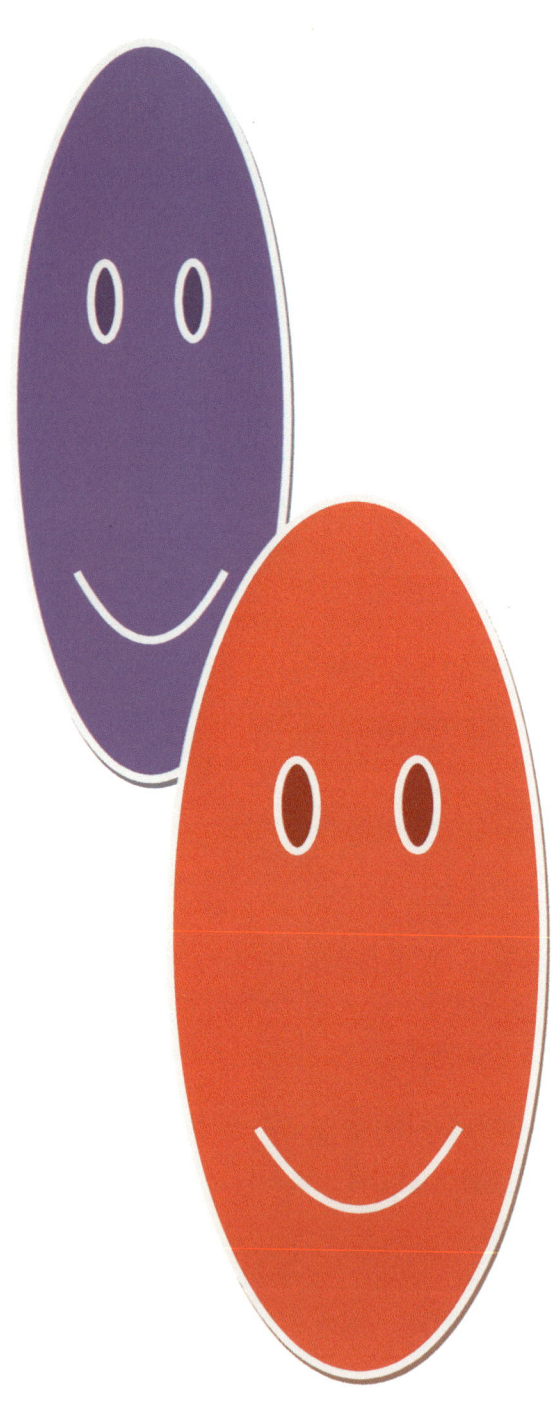

Managing Director: When is the delegation arriving?

General Manager: In three hours.

Managing Director: Is everything agreed in the contract.

General Manager: All but two points.

Managing Director: What discount did we give on our standard price?

General Manager: Twenty percent.

Managing Director: What are the two outstanding points?

General Manager: We pay fifty thousand dollars for each day of delay caused by us and they pay ten thousand dollars for each day of delay caused by them.

Managing Director: This sounds unfair. What is their argument?

General Manager: They claim we are their only supplier for this product while they are one of many clients for us. They are concerned that we

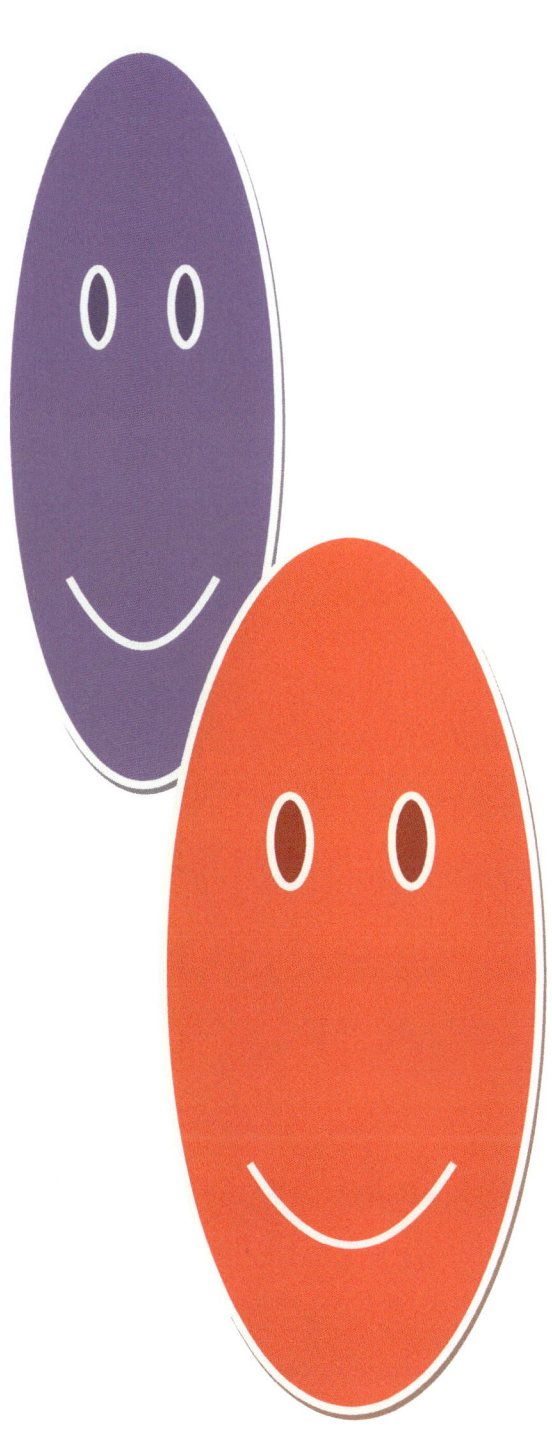

will give delivery priority to other clients at their expense.

Managing Director: Who decides which of the two parties is responsible for the delay?

General Manager: They do.

Managing Director: What are the positions of our managers?

General Manager: It is evenly split. Sales and operations recommend we agree, while legal and finance recommend we reject.

Managing Director: What is your position?

General Manager: I am told by operations that they see no reason why they should not be able to deliver on time. I therefore support the deal.

Managing Director: Have the negotiations on this matter been exhausted or is there room for further negotiations.

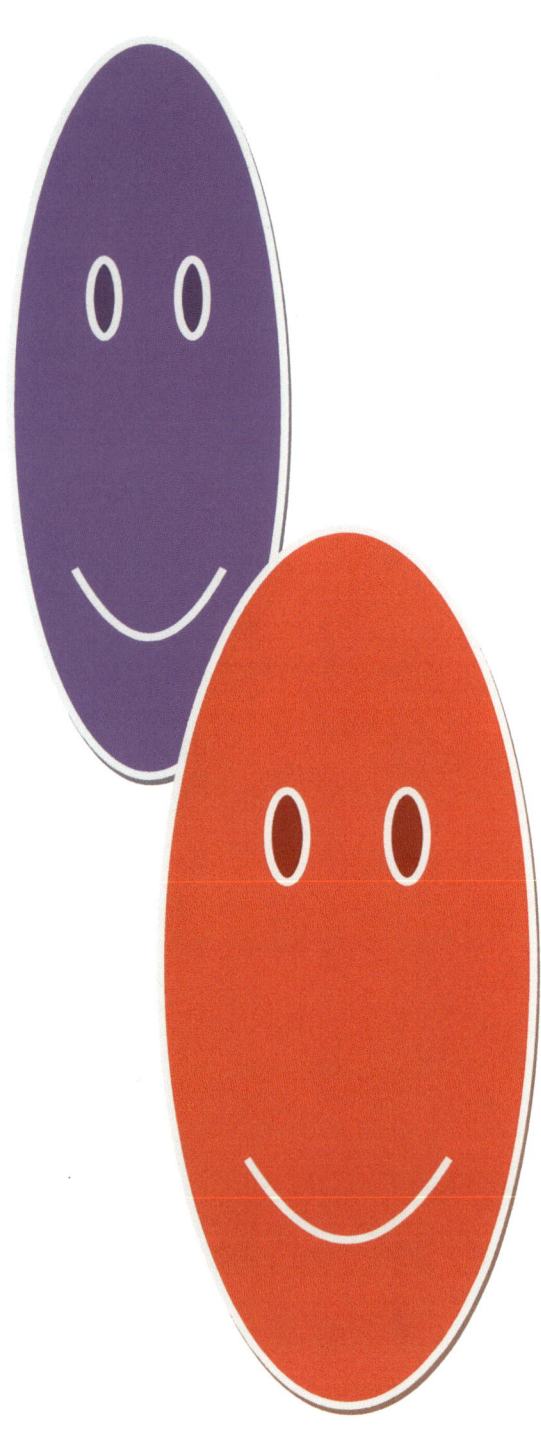

General Manager: The delegation that is coming has no authority to alter this deal only to sign it.

Managing Director: Who are you planning should see them?

General Manager: You, I our sales manager and our operations manager.

(The Managing Director then slaps the General Manager hard on his right cheek)

General Manager: ARE YOU CRAZY? WHY DID YOU SLAP ME ON THE FACE YOU IDIOT?

Managing Director: Calm down. I am just checking that you believe in what you preach.

General Manager: WHAT AM I PREACHING YOU IMBICILE?

Managing Director: In business terms; you just advised me that if someone strikes me on my right cheek I should turn to him the other.

Cow 1: Did you hear about the new milk and cheese factory that is opening in town?

Cow 2: Yes I did. Are you planning to apply for a job there?

Cow 1: Yes. How about you?

Cow 2: Me too; although I am told that the competition will be strong and the interviews are quite tough.

Cow 1: Do you know what the interviews will involve?

Cow 2: Apparently most of the factory's output is for export. Therefore aside from the standard test of milking us to check our output; there are language tests to make sure our milk can be exported. You need to speak two additional languages aside from your native mooing.

Cow 1: How many foreign languages do you speak?

Cow 2: None.

Cow 1: How about you?

Cow 2: None

Cow 1: What do you think we should do?

Cow 2: Fake it; but make sure that you smile and wink all the time.

Cow 1: How will that help?

Cow 2: I understand that the human owners of the factory have recruited three bulls to do the language tests for the applicants. I think they can be bribed with favours.

Cow 1: Would that not be cheating?

Cow 2: I am a cow. All I know is how to give milk and how to please bulls. Suddenly out of the blue I am supposed to know two additional languages otherwise I cannot be employed. What am I supposed to do go to school?

Key: Have you seen my brother?

Key Chain: What is his name?

Key: His name is Rambo. He is trained to open any door.

Key Chain: Trained by whom?

Key: He never says and refuses to discuss this part of his life.

Key Chain: What does he look like?

Key: He has a round green head and is marked by a golden stripe on his stem and has a red tip.

Key Chain: I have never seen him.

Key: I know he was on some secret assignment but I do not know where. My Mother is very worried.

Key Chain: I really cannot help. I will ask around; but I doubt if any of my key chain friends would know him. Only keys that open one door hang on key chains.

Interviewer: What is your name?

Job Applicant: Any name that this job needs me to have.

Interviewer: I meant the name on your birth certificate?

Job Applicant: Do not worry about my birth certificate. I am happy to change the name written on it by Deed Poll to the name this job requires me to have.

Interviewer: Relax. Nobody would disqualify you from taking the job because of your name.

Job Applicant: That is what you all say at the beginning. Then you hear my name and you politely say that the job is taken.

Interviewer: Look I cannot process your application if I do not know your name.

Job Applicant: I am happy to work for you; I am happy to accept any name you give me; I am happy to make that name my official name by

Deed Poll; why are you not satisfied with all that?

Interviewer: What was your name in your last job?

Job Applicant: Number Seven.

Interviewer: The job before that?

Job Applicant: Number Sixteen

Interviewer: This is crazy. What did they call you at school?

Job Applicant: Number Twenty Three.

Interviewer: Was it normal to have numbers instead of names in your last jobs?

Job Applicant: Yes.

Interviewer: What were your previous two jobs?

Job Applicant: Cook and assistant cook in a Chinese Takeaway.

Woman (*passing by*): Why are you standing on your head on the pavement?

Man: To make a statement.

Woman: What statement?

Man: The world does not understand me?

Woman: What do you want the world to understand?

Man: I am underpaid, overworked and should have a better wife.

Woman: Assuming I accept your statement and I am part of this world what do you expect me to do?

Man: From you, I expect nothing.

Woman: Why?

Man: If you have the time and the inclination to stand and talk with someone standing on his head on the pavement, then your ability to deliver any change to my life is doubtful.

Doctor: You claim you have a business plan which is the reason you say you do not wish to be employed. What is your business plan?

Man: I prepare myself for destiny to deliver.

Doctor: What do you mean?

Man: My uncle is rich. I am his only heir. On the basis of past experience I expect destiny to deliver my inheritance to me. I therefore do not wish to be distracted and want to remain focused on the business opportunity I identified.

Doctor: But suppose you die before your uncle?

Man: Every business has its own risks.

Doctor: Suppose his will excludes you?

Man: Any business expects to have competitors.

Man 1: Why are those three students running in a circle?

Man 2: The first is studying philosophy. He is running to understand the meaning of life.

Man 1: How about the second one?

Man 2: He is an engineer. He is running to improve the quality of life.

Man 1: What about the third one?

Man 2: He is a theology student. His is running to protect the after-life.

Man 1: What is the man sitting in the middle of the circle doing?

Man 2: Nobody knows. He just sits there and smiles.

Judge: Why do you think we should imprison him and not you?

Business Owner: Because he was my advisor.

Judge: Did he not advise you not to proceed with the fraudulent scheme that led to the trouble you are in?

Business Owner: Yes he did.

Judge: Did he not advise you of the consequences if you were caught?

Business Owner: Yes he did.

Judge: So why should he be imprisoned and not you?

Business Owner: Because he refused to advise me how not to get caught.

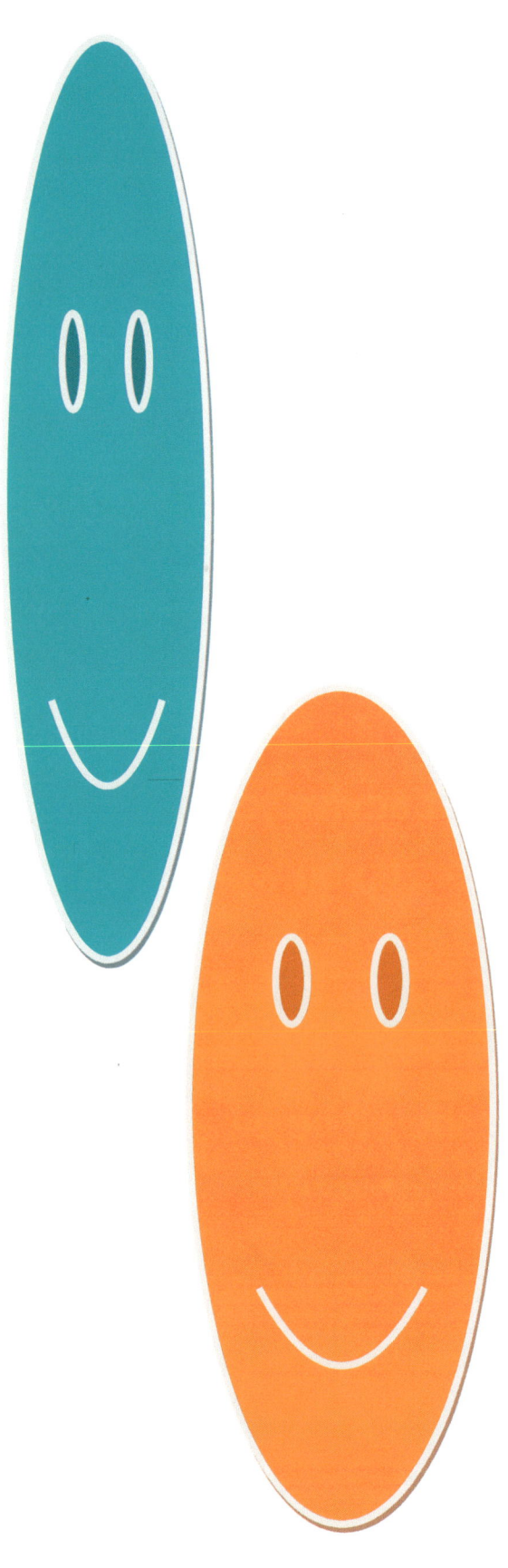

Traveller 1: What are you reading?

Traveller 2: Dante's Inferno.

Traveller 1: Interesting. Do you think sin can be categorised in order of severity?

Traveller 2: I do. For example killing is a more serious sin than stealing.

Traveller 1: So you consider the degree of harm a sin does to others puts a value on its severity.

Traveller 2: Yes.

Traveller 1: Do you also consider that within the same sin there are degrees of severity?

Traveller 2: What do you mean?

Traveller 1: Take for example betrayal. Do you consider a wife's betrayal of her husband; a partner betraying his business partner and a citizen's betrayal of his country all of equal value?

Traveller 2: No. A betrayal of a citizen of his country is a much worse sin.

Traveller 1: So; you consider both the harm a sin does to others and the number of people harmed in that sin a guideline to the severity of the sin; is that your position?

Traveller 2: Yes.

Traveller 1: Ok let's eliminate those two variables. Is a wife betraying her husband after he betrayed her less sinful than if he had not betrayed her?

Traveller 2: I suppose so.

Traveller 1: So in addition to the harm a sin does, the number of people it affects you also consider the circumstances under which a sin is committed relevant to its severity.

Traveller 2: Yes that is correct.

Traveller 1: How about frequency? In our example if the husband betrayed his wife once and she went ahead and betrayed him three times does that make her sin more severe?

Traveller 2: I suppose so. What do you think?

Traveller 1: I am not the one reading the book.

Traveller 2: But you must have an opinion?

Traveller 1: My opinion is simple; in matters of theology other people's opinion of sin does not matter; in matters of law they do.

Traveller 2: So you think I should not read Dante's Inferno?

Traveller 1: I do not know what you should do; all I know is I read it three times and enjoyed it immensely.

Traveller 2: What lesson did you learn from the book?

Traveller 1: Human imagination is the most magical gift God gave to man.

Deputy Managing Director: Why every time an employee comes to your office you leave your chair and sit on the floor?

Managing Director: Why do you ask?

Deputy Managing Director: Because the employees feel embarrassed so they thank you and leave.

Managing Director: What happens to the problem they came to see me about?

Deputy Managing Director: I do not know. I suppose they either solve it or it was not a problem in the first place.

Managing Director: Do they come and see you after they leave me?

Deputy Managing Director: No.

Managing Director: Would you sit on the floor if they came to see you?

Deputy Managing Director: No.

Managing Director: Maybe if you do they may come and see you.

Sales Lady: That will be fifty five dollars Sir.

Customer: Do you take credit cards?

Sales Lady: Sorry; our credit card machine is not working.

Customer: I am not carrying that much cash.

Sales Lady: The wallet in your shirt pocket seems bulging with cash?

Customer: No it is full of photos.

Sales Lady: Your wife's?

Customer: Well to start with it was my wife; two sons and my daughter. Then my wife said it would be nice if I included her parents; so I did. My Mother saw my wallet and was surprised it did not include her and Dad's pictures so I added them. My wife then felt that under the circumstances I should also include our daughter's fiancée; which I did. My daughter in law heard about that, complained to my son, so I had to include her picture.

Sales Lady: What about your other son's wife?

Customer: Well he is not married yet. So I use this free space in my wallet to carry my credit card which does not leave any room for cash.

Sales Lady: May I make a parctical suggestion?

Customer: Go ahead.

Sales Lady: Why don't you memorise all their pictures and then you do not need to carry them around. If at any time you forget how any of them looks like you can call him or her and ask them to come and see you immediately wherever they are.

Customer: You think that will work?

Sales Lady: I hope it does otherwise as the number of your grand children increases you will have a serious problem with the size of your wallet.

Client: My name is Chafcheer; Ms. Noonoo, my fiancée, said that you can make me look informed and a deep thinker.

Consultant: Yes we can cure your defects in that regard. We specialise in offering our clients a set of opinions that they can use on various subjects. We offer you the verbal tools to enable you to bring the subjects you have an opinion on into a conversation. It is a total package.

Client: How do I select the opinions?

Consultant: We have a menu version and an al carte version. The first is an off the shelf package that has been used before; the second is tailor made for you only. It goes without saying that the al carte is more expensive.

Client: How many opinions you think I should have?

Consultant: This depends on who you are trying to impress. We think

that nineteen opinions would be more than enough provided you do not see the same people more than twice; or if you do see them more you do not care if they are impressed or not. We also suggest you update your set of opinions once every six months.

Client: My memory is not that good. Nineteen opinions are too much to memorise. Ms. Noonoo said you have a deluxe package.

Consultant: Yes. We call it "Brain on the Move". It involves you wearing a transmitter and receiver. One of our operatives is always about two hundred and seventy meters away from you. She hears everything you hear and advises you what you should answer or say.

Client: Just like my fiancée! How do you charge for that package?

Consultant: One hundred and fifty dollars per hour.

Client: My fiancée charges fifty!

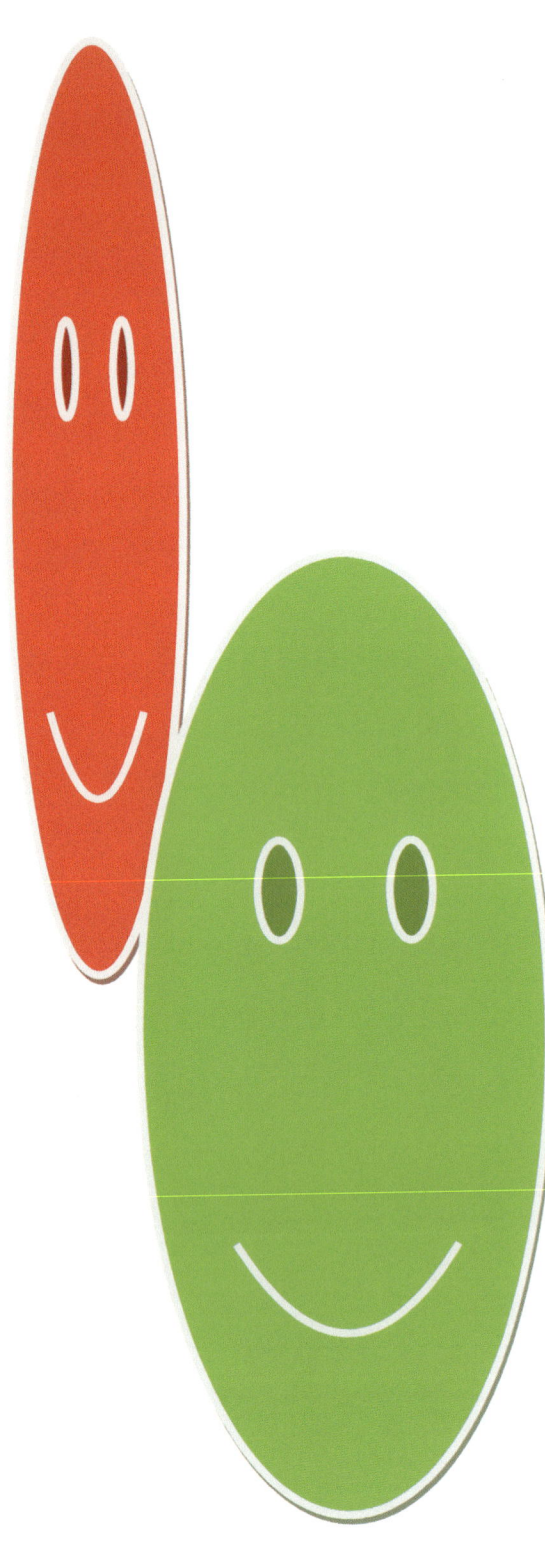

Man 1: What's your hobby?

Man 2: Playing Golf. How about you?

Man 1: Travelling.

Man 2: Do you travel by plane or ship?

Man 1: Neither. I am scared from flying and I get sea sick in ships.

Man 2: Is it by car or train then?

Man 1: Neither. I get car sick and have a phobia from trains.

Man 2: So how do you travel?

Man 1: I spend three days every six weeks watching films about a country; on those days I only eat the food of that country and employ

someone who is a native of that country to spend three hours with me on each day.

Man 2: But that way you have no true experience of that country and no memories to carry with you?

Man 1: I address that by arranging for a local photographer I know to produce various photographs of me on locations from that country through a scanning technology he has.

Man 2: But that is an illusion of travel not true travel?

Man 1: How would I know the difference? I have never travelled except that way.

Interviewer: Do you have the disciplined mind this job demands?

Applicant: Yes I think I do.

Interviewer: I have to ask you questions to make sure you do. Do you agree to undertake the test?

Applicant: Yes I agree.

Interviewer: We remotely monitor your eye movements to ensure that you are giving true answers? Do you agree with that procedure?

Applicant: Yes.

Interviewer: Do you visit your friends in alphabetical order?

Applicant: No.

Interviewer: Do you file the greeting cards you receive?

Applicant: No

Interviewer: Are you intimate with your wife on a pre-defined day and time?

Applicant: No.

Interviewer: Do you consider having options a negative thing?

Applicant: No

Interviewer: Do you prefer dreaming to thinking?

Applicant: No.

Interviewer: Do you find it difficult to use the word "yes" all the time?

Applicant: Yes.

Interviewer: I am afraid you are not suitable for the job.

Applicant: Why not?

Interviewer: Your answers indicate that you are too wild. We are a traditional company. The last person who did this job was dead for two days before anyone realised it.

Applicant: I am surprised that you did not ask him to carry on with the job regardless?

Brush: Hi; who are you?

Hair Spray: My name is Hair Spray. I have recently joined this salon.

Brush: What do you do?

Hair Spray: I ensure that your artwork once it is finished is protected and preserved.

Brush: How do you do that?

Hair Spray: Putting it bluntly I glue it in place; although I have all sorts of scientific language that I can use to impress your client with.

Brush: But your action could in the long term cause the canvass on which I do my artwork to fall?

Hair Spray: Maybe; all you should care about is that when your artwork leaves your office it is perfectly preserved; what happens after that is not your concern. We, my friend, are in the image business neither yesterday nor tomorrow matters to us.

Tuxedo: Is it true that your boss never joins gatherings of any sort?

Jeans: He does not join some type of gatherings?

Tuxedo: Which type he would refuse to attend?

Jeans: Weddings; funerals; birthdays; receptions; lunch or dinner parties; and any home or office gathering of any nature.

Tuxedo: That is quite a list. What gathering would he attend?

Jeans: Any other gathering where his presence or absence is irrelevant to those present and where no one would bother to greet him or care to talk to him.

Tuxedo: Are there any such gatherings?

Jeans: Of course. Movies; theatre; opera; parks; shopping malls; libraries; take away restaurants; fun fairs; sports games; music concerts.

145

Wife: Why are you silent?

Husband: Why do you say I am?

Wife: You have not said a word in the last two hours.

Husband: That does not mean I am silent. All it means is that the loud screaming and shouting that is taking place in my brain has not yet transferred itself to my tongue

Wife: Does that process take long?

Husband: It depends. My tongue is an unreliable creature. If you give it half baked ideas or unpolished sentences it proceeds to use them in a very stupid and offending way.

Wife: Is that not the natural way things happen?

Husband: It is one way that things could happen.

Wife: But if everybody did what you do it will take hours to talk?

Husband: Probably; but as with everything between us, a compromise is always possible.

Snake: Why all this fuss? All I did was tell that stupid Eve to eat the apple. Did I force her to eat the apple? Did I hold a gun to her silly head? I did nothing of the sort. All I did was express an opinion. I thought freedom of speech was protected by all constitutions? Why am I being so mistreated?

Shark: Calm down. I have never seen you so angry before. You normally move quietly. Why raise an issue now which is centuries old?

Snake: It easy for you to talk. You go about your business happily killing and eating Eve's children and grand children; does anybody cast you as a symbol of evil and deceit? No as a matter of fact they make films about you. I, on the other hand, am continuously cursed by them just because I believe in free speech.

Shark: I see. This is all about the three films I did: Jaws1, Jaws 2 and Jaws 3. You are just jealous.

Snake: It is not a question of jealous it is a question of fairness. Why should you a killer make films and receive royalties while I only receive insults? Even the damn apple that I suggested Eve should eat ends up owning one of the world's biggest technological companies. This is not justice at all.

Shark: You had a role in the film Jungle Book so why complain?

Snake: Do not be silly. You call those few scenes they gave me a role. Any way it was a cartoon character and you know very well they pay no royalties to a cartoon character only to the voice over artist.

Shark: So all this boils down to money?

Snake: No it is about free speech and not being punished for expressing one's opinion. Although if they do pay me royalties for every occasion they curse me, then it becomes easier being their symbol of deceit and evil.

Vote: Who are you and what are you doing here?

Veto: My name is Veto; I am here to block what you lot might agree on.

Vote: What do you mean block? You mean you make your choice like the rest of us and a majority decides an issue.

Veto: It seems you are new here. If I decide against something it does not happen.

Vote: What makes you so special?

Veto: Have you heard of the cartoon Popeye? He is the guy who when he is upset; eats spinach; becomes very powerful and crushes his enemy.

Vote: What does that have to do with you having the right to block what the majority of us wish to happen?

Veto: A decision against my will has the same effect on me as spinach has on Popeye.

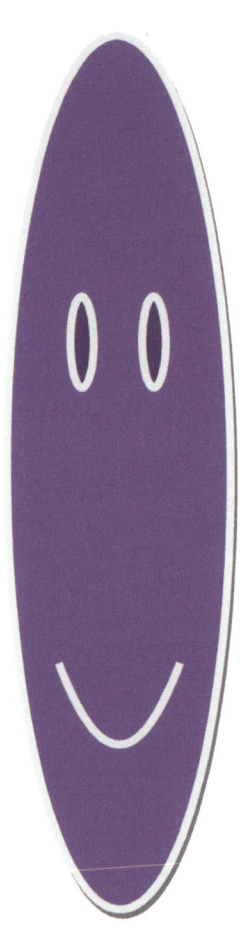

Ant 1: I see no reason why the Committee was so hard on me. I found the food I was asked to locate; I left the necessary trace; it is not my fault that the designated team that was supposed to follow got lost.

Ant 2: You are the point man and when the trace is lost they hold you accountable. You know how we ants are obsessed with efficiency and organisation

Ant 1: I did not ask to be the point man. I did stress to them that I did leave the trace. I believe however that the trace was erased by a traitor.

Ant 2: You are the point man because they know you are the best. This does not mean that you do not make mistakes.

Ant 1: I am the last person to say anybody does not make mistakes. My issue is that they prefer to doubt my efficiency than face the horrible prospect that there is a traitor among us. I know what I did; I left

the correct trace as I have done hundreds of times before.

Ant 2: This was a big mountain of food we lost and we are very close to winter. You have to understand why the Committee was so upset.

Ant 1: I am upset too. I found that food mountain and worked very hard to do so. You would expect them to come down hard on the follow-up team leader for failing to track the trace rather than me.

Ant 2: But you know he is very good in tracking traces?

Ant 1: That is why I keep saying it is sabotage. The Committee is still living in the old ages. They think all ants accept that they are equal; happy to share food equally and would not betray each other for additional food. That may have been our grandfathers' attitude but things have changed and the Committee must recognise that and plan for it.

Promoter: But the song you intend to sing is in a foreign language to that spoken by the majority of the audience today. How would they understand that the song is a call for freedom?

Singer: I wrote the song; I will be singing it and I will say it is about freedom.

Promoter: But how would they know?

Singer: They know who I am; they know what I did and if that is not enough then I do not deserve to write or sing songs. The audience can kick me of the stage and I will not feel offended.

Promoter: But you have written the same song, whose words are beautiful, in their language; why sing it in the foreign language?

Singer: Because the language in which I will sing it in is that spoken by those who are yet to become free.

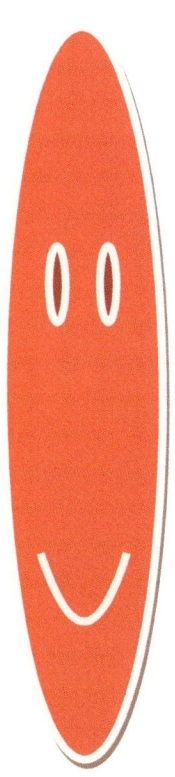

Surveyor: If I understand you correctly, your position is that because your Grandfather built the one hundred and fifty stone steps that lead to the mouth of the cave; then usage of these steps cannot take place without your permission.

Land Owner: Correct.

Surveyor: You do agree though that the cave itself is public property.

Land Owner: Yes.

Surveyor: You also agree that the section of the mountain that the steps were built on were originally public land but were purchased from the state by your grandfather prior to anybody knowing that the cave is there.

Land Owner: Correct.

Surveyor: You do recognise that there is no other way for us to build alternative steps because of the nature of the mountain.

Land Owner: If you say so.

153

Surveyor: You therefore accept that this makes the cave as if it was privately owned by you.

Land Owner: It is not owned by me.

Surveyor: How would we access it without your permission?

Land Owner: You can access it any time you wish as long as you do not use my steps.

Surveyor: But nobody can get up there through any other way except it seems the eagles that fly to nest there.

Land Owner: If you say so.

Surveyor: Do you not want that people go up there and enjoy the beauty of that cave?

Land Owner: I personally have no opinion either way; but if I was an eagle my answer would be no.

Son: Dad, does a magician have special powers?

Dad: Yes.

Son: Is it in the stick he normally holds?

Dad: The stick is just one of many tools?

Son: What are his other tools?

Dad: His hands and mouth.

Son: What is his power called?

Dad: Illusion.

Son: Where does it come from?

Dad: His imagination.

Son: How does it work?

Dad: He makes us look in the wrong direction and does what he wants to do without us noticing; the gullible of us call it magic.

Son: How many magicians are there?

Dad: On stage a few; off stage millions.

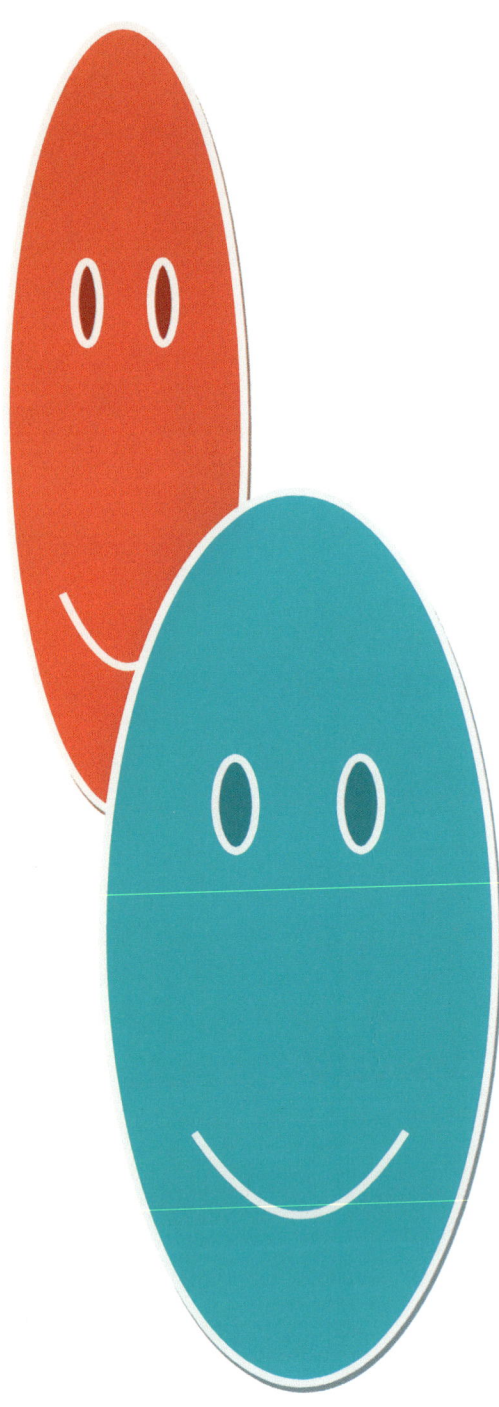

Friend 1: Is there a possibility that you can forgive him?

Friend 2: It depends?

Friend 1: Depends on what?

Friend 2: If you mean not pursuing matters through the courts then that is possible; if you mean restoring the relationship then that is impossible.

Friend 1: Why the distinction?

Friend 2: Withdrawing my claims from the court is humanly feasible and therefore possible.

Friend 1: Surely returning things back to normal is also your decision and therefore also possible?

Friend 2: No that involves violating the universal Humpty Dumpty law which is logically not possible.

Friend 1: What is that universal law?

Friend 2: Trust once broken can never be repaired.

Player 1: Everybody knows that chess is a superior game. It involves brain power alone. Therefore when your opponent is defeated your victory is complete because he cannot claim any outside factors such as the throw of the dice that you have to face in backgammon.

Player 2: I grant you that a win over a single opponent in chess cannot be explained away except as due to the superiority of the winner; but it is a win over one person unlike the case of backgammon.

Player 1: What do you mean? There are only two players in backgammon also.

Player 2: No there are three players: you; your opponent; and the dice.

Player 1: How can the dice be a player?

Player 2: He actively represents the greatest player of them all, namely destiny.

Clergyman: What do you do all day when there is no war?

Soldier: Train for one.

Clergyman: Suppose it did not happen?

Soldier: No true soldier ever wishes for a war to happen.

Clergyman: So you train to participate in something that you wish would not happen but you are ready if it does?

Soldier: Yes. How about you?

Clergyman: In my case the war is ongoing all the time. What I do is train myself and others for the day the war will be over.

Acquaintance 1: What line of work are you in?

Acquaintance 2: I work for a TV station that provides twenty four hour news coverage.

Acquaintance 1: Are you a reporter or presenter?

Acquaintance 2: Neither. I am a background researcher.

Acquaintance 1: What do you research?

Acquaintance 2: Whenever a war breaks out somewhere it is my job to find out how the names of the towns and cities in that country are pronounced.

Acquaintance 1: How do you do that then?

Acquaintance 2: I have to call at least five locals in that country get them to pronounce the name of a specific town or city; feed

their pronunciation into our computer and produce digitally the appropriate pronunciation. I then need to ensure that our correspondents and presenters learn how to pronounce the names correctly.

Acquaintance 1: This sounds fun. Is there any downside to such a job?

Acquaintance 2: If you do not mind the occasional insult and abuse then I would say no.

Acquaintance 1: Why would the locals insult you when you call?

Acquaintance 2: No they do not. As a matter of fact they seem happy that I bother to call them at all. The abuse I get is from our correspondents and presenters when they find that some of the names of these towns and cities are difficult to pronounce.

Box: Who are you?

Ring: I am a circular metal that is worn on different parts of the human body.

Box: I have heard of you. I understand you have different sizes, you can be made from different metals, and you could have all sorts of stones attached to you.

Ring: Yes. The stones are meaningless except to show if a person is rich. My size is dictated by where I am worn; which then defines the message.

Box: So what's the message when you are worn on the second figure of the left hand?

Ring: "This person is taken. Do not tempt her with any offers."

Box: How about when you are worn on the ear?

Ring: "I listen and obey."

Box: What is the message when you are worn round the ankle?

Ring: "I am chained to my environment."

Box: I am told that there are some that wear you on their nose. Is that true?

Ring: Yes.

Box: What is the message?

Ring: "I am stupid and can be lead anywhere by the nose."

Box: Do all your users know about these messages?

Ring: No; a few do but the majority think we are only decorative ornaments.

Box: Why don't you tell them?

Ring: I doubt they would care.

Pawn (*Chess*): I understand that if I reach the last row safely I can convert myself to any chess item I wish.

Chessboard: Anything but the king; it is strategically logical to change yourself to a queen; this will give you maximum strength.

Pawn: Why can't I convert myself to a king?

Chessboard: Because I can have only one king sitting on me; but there is no limit however to the number of queens that can live on my surface.

Pawn: Don't you have any problems with the women liberation movement?

Chessboard: Non to date.

Pawn: Have you been sued under the sex discrimination act?

Chessboard: No.

Pawn: Have you been sued under the equal opportunities act?

Chessboard: No.

Pawn: Have you been sued under the discrimination at work act?

Chessboard: No.

Pawn: For someone who has been playing by the rules for many hundreds of years, you seem to ignore quite a lot of prevailing laws that specifically prohibit you from implementing the conversion conditions you are imposing on me.

Chessboard: Do these laws apply to me?

Pawn: You are asking me? I am just a simple pawn. I suggest you find yourself a good lawyer.

Accountant: I know you make a lot of donations to charity but you never allow me to claim them on your behalf against your tax bill; why?

Businessman: It is not charity if I deduct it from my tax bill; it is equivalent to me instructing the Government as to which third party it should spend its tax money on. I have no such mandate.

Accountant: I respect your principles however this does not make business sense. I know that in any business transaction you would not let one penny escape you if you consider it your right.

Businessman: Because I am a good businessman I refuse to expose my business activities to my charitable activities. This will

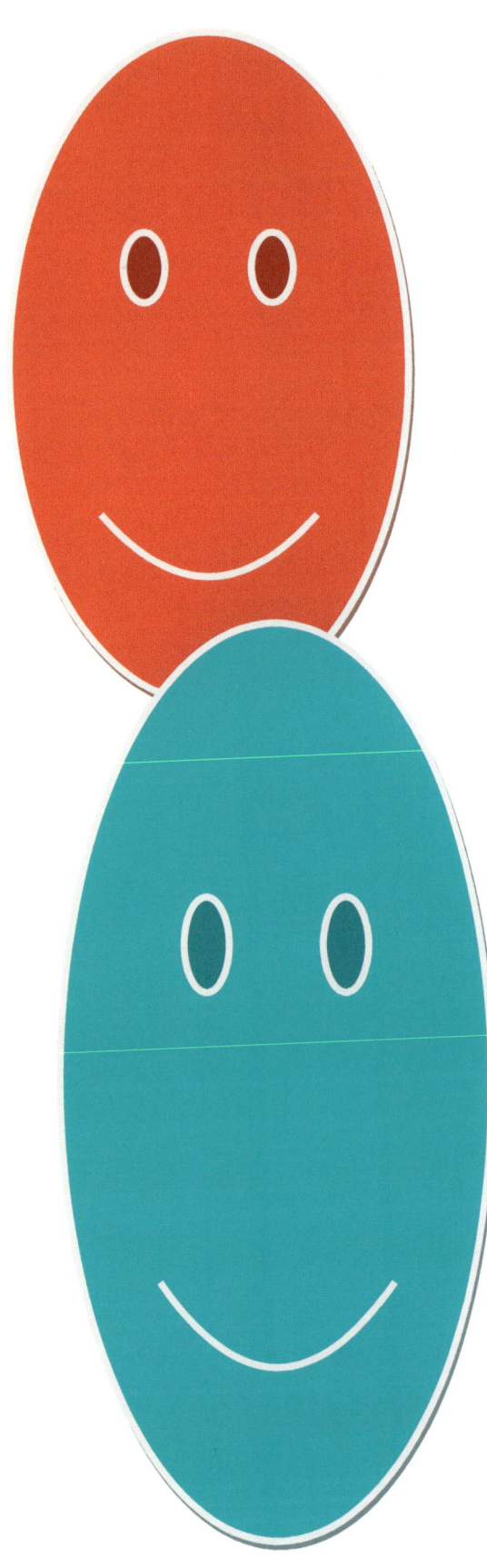

cause the former to learn bad habits.

Accountant: Ok; how about making the donation public at least that will give some free publicity to the business?

Businessman: The donor's anonymity is the shield that protects the recipient's pride. That pride is more valuable than any donation I give.

Accountant: Ok; how about allowing the recipient to name the donor? Surely that has no impact on the principles you outlined?

Businessman: Anybody who agrees to sell his pride for a donation is not somebody I wish to donate to.

Train Traveller 1: Have you met my second cousin on my Mother's side?

Train Traveller 2: No.

Train Traveller 1: He would very much like to meet you.

Train Traveller 2: Why?

Train Traveller 1: He has heard so much about you.

Train Traveller 2: From whom?

Train Traveller 1: From me of course.

Train Traveller 2: Why would you talk about me to him?

Train Traveller 1: Because you are my friend and so is he.

Train Traveller 2: Why do you consider me your friend?

Train Traveller 1: We daily take the same train trip; you are always polite and whenever we

talk you are very knowledgeable on the subject we talk about.

Train Traveller 2: What was the main subject we talked about in the past six months?

Train Traveller 1: The importance of anonymity and privacy.

Train Traveller 2: Did you understand their importance based on what I explained?

Train Traveller 1: Yes.

Train Traveller 2: Did you outline my arguments to your second cousin on your Mother's side?

Train Traveller 1: Yes.

Train Traveller 2: I have no doubt you did an excellent job in explaining my position; this eliminates my need to meet with him. Well done.

Book Inspector: It has come to our attention that your book is introducing new ideas that were not previously cleared by us?

Author: I am writing about freedom of choice.

Book Inspector: Such new concepts if not properly communicated would make ordinary people ask questions for which my bosses have not yet found answers.

Author: Is that a bad thing?

Book Inspector: Yes; questions have a way of breeding other questions?

Author: What do you suggest I do?

Book Inspector: Write a book about cleaning cooking utensils and I will ensure that one hundred thousand copies are

bought by the Institute of Food Hygiene.

Author: But I know nothing about cleaning cooking utensils?

Book Inspector: What's the problem with that? I have been in my job for twenty five years and I know nothing about books.

Author: So how do you decide which book to approve and which to ban?

Book Inspector: That is easy. Each year I have a subject authorised by my bosses; books on that subject are permitted. This year it is cooking utensils. Last year it was chiropody and the year before it was sheep.

Author: But not many people would read them?

Book Inspector: I have no problem with that.

Priest: This is the fourth time this week you come to fix the electricity in the Church; how can that be?

Electrician: My Mother, who attends your Church, informs me that God has a purpose for everything. May be through these electricity breakdowns you keep having God is testing your patience?

Priest: My Bishop agrees with you that I am being tested; although he has a different theory as to what I am being tested for?

Electrician: What is his theory then?

Priest: He believes that I am being tested to see if I know

how to choose a good electrician?

Electrician: Which of the two theories do you support?

Priest: After preying and carefully thinking about it I decided that both theories are correct.

Electrician: How can that be?

Priest: I believe I was tested for my patience and I passed with flying colours; I was however also tested by God for my ability to choose good electricians and regrettably I failed miserably.

Wife: I want….

Husband: That is fine.

Wife: But I did not tell you what it is I want?

Husband: That makes no difference.

Wife: How can it not make a difference?

Husband: I know who you are and what you deserve; you know who I am and what I can deliver; the rest is all details that can be discussed at leisure; after all we have a life time to do that.

Sister: Where are you going so late at night?

Brother: To thank Samuel for his contribution to our charity.

Sister: But more than two hundred people contributed today and Samuel's contribution was the smallest of the lot? Why him?

Brother: He gave the most as a percentage of what he earns.

Sister: How does that help our charity; what we are after are major contributions. I suggest you focus on those who are able to donate serious money so that we can help the largest number of those who are in need.

Brother: Charity my dear is a state of mind; to give when you don't have is its true measure. What you are describing is business; of that I am ignorant.

Research Director: You want my people to invent a pill that makes the "father to be" feel all the symptoms the "mother to be" feels throughout the nine months?

Marketing Director: Yes plus feeling all the pains of "giving birth".

Research Director: You think there is a market for such a pill?

Marketing Director: Yes; my people think the market will be big.

Research Director: Who will be your clients?

Marketing Director: We believe there will be three categories of clients: the first are husbands who cannot explain to their wives why they do not share the pain if they expect to share the pleasure of a growing family; the second are wives who wish to do a dry run before they commit to getting pregnant;

Research Director: These two categories cannot be that big a market?

Marketing Director: I agree. The biggest market is Governments wanting to cause smokers to quit but does not know how.

Research Director: How does this pill help?

Marketing Director: The Government will force every tobacco company to put a powdered version of your pill at the inhaling tip of each cigarette which gets immediately absorbed through the skin.

Research Director: Would that not be illegal?

Marketing Director: Why? The Government already writes on every cigarette box that smoking kills; why would an additional ingredient concern the smoker?

Research Director: But it will cause them pain?

Marketing Director: No more than the pain any woman, who could become pregnant, would have to endure.

Research Director: Is that fair to the smoker?

Marketing Director: If God thinks it is fair to have such a pain for a good cause so should the Government.

Research Director: Do you think you will get the necessary political support to pass such legislation?

Marketing Director: Of course politicians love to have God on their side.

Wife: I do not understand why you are so worried? This report from the clinic is not yours. It is in somebody else's name and the date of birth is different than yours.

Husband: But it shows our address.

Wife: That could be a mistake.

Husband: Yes; but the mistake could be that the name and date of birth are wrong and the address is the correct part of the report.

Wife: We will know tomorrow when the clinic opens up. There is nothing we can do tonight.

Husband: We can call emergency services again.

Wife: What would they tell you the second time that they did not already say to you when you called the first time? The reports from the clinic do not show on their computer. Like us they can do nothing in terms of finding out if the report is yours before the clinic opens.

Husband: You want me to sit here and do nothing?

Wife: Let us assume that the report was yours; what would you be doing now?

Husband: Do the scan the letter says I am supposed to do.

Wife: According to this letter, when is the scan booked for?

Husband: two days from now.

Wife: So you would be still sitting and doing nothing?

Husband: No I would be sitting worrying about what the scan would say rather than worry, as I am doing now, if I really need a scan or not.

Wife: Which is the worse of the two worries?

Husband (*thinking*): The second I suppose.

Wife: Fine. Shut up and go to sleep.

Assistant: You're Excellency everybody was surprised by your sudden departure. The fifty thousand crowds were cheering your name. Nobody understood why you just stood up left.

Prime Minister: What happened after I left?

Assistant: The crowd went quiet and each of your Ministers took the podium and explained the plans for his ministry.

Prime Minister: Where they all cheered all the time like I was?

Assistant: No.

Prime Minister: Where they booed all the time?

Assistant: No; as they explained their plans there were cheering and booing depending on what was being said regarding each issue.

Prime Minister: Then I succeeded.

Assistant: I do not understand your Excellency?

Prime Minister: The crowd were cheering for me continuously with the expectation that I can solve all their problems alone. The truth is I cannot. All I can do is to choose competent Ministers and allow them to develop and implement plans agreed by Cabinet.

Assistant: But people want one leader. If you vacate that role others may fill it.

Prime Minister: Those others will face the same limitations I do and unless their plans are better than mine they will be kicked out in due course.

Assistant: But that is not sound politics on your part; in our business tomorrow has no value except as a parking lot for promises.

Prime Minister: I agree; but if I allow the cheers to continue I will one day succumb to the deadly illusion that I alone do matter and my opinions are always right. Nothing could be worse for any nation.

Club Chairman: I do not see why we are investing so much in creating three reserve teams each of which is equivalent in capability to the first team?

Club Manager: You notice that all my three reserve teams are always in full gear and sitting in the benches just behind the substitution reserves that are entitled to play during a match.

Club Chairman: Yes; you do that while you and I know very well they cannot play in that game.

Club Manager: There presence is not for the purpose of playing but to intimidate the other team by sending a warning message.

Club Chairman: What warning message?

Club Manager: My message says: "We can match you injury for injury; however we have a much greater capacity than you in replacing our injured players for future games."

Greed: Stop interfering with my customers. You are hurting my business. I will not take that calmly.

Satisfied: I did nothing of the sort. Some of your customers, once they become aware of my "enough" pill, decide to try it. Many find that it helps them to relax and enjoy life more.

Greed: The campaign for your "enough" pill is financed by people with religious intentions.

Satisfied: The campaign for your "more and more" syrup is financed by people with profit motivations.

Greed: You want people to slow down and become lazy.

Satisfied: You want them to keep running and die prematurely.

Greed: How about meeting half way?

Satisfied: This is fine by me.

Greed: Ok; let's meet after your holiday.

Politician 1: Stop using Boyle's Law for gas on our people.

Politician 2: What do you mean?

Politician 1: Well Boyle viewed all the molecules of a gas as identical and showed that by putting pressure on them you can squeeze them into smaller containers; your housing policy for the poor is the same.

Politician 2: With the limited resources of our nation do you have any alternative aside from using Charles Law?

Politician 1: What do you mean?

Politician 2: According to Charles the molecules of a gas are also identical and when you apply heat they start agitating and expanding the volume they occupy; is that not what you are doing by causing the poor to riot in the streets.

Politician 1: How about a chemical truce? I will ask Charles to keep quiet and you try to make Boyle change his ways?

Asset: Please Doctor I need your help. I think I am starting to have multiple-schizophrenia.

Psychiatrist: OK; calm down. What is the problem?

Asset: I live in a town called Balance Sheet; have you heard of it?

Psychiatrist: Yes.

Asset: Well in my town there is a gang of accountants who force me to act different roles for their amusement. Each role is more complex than the other. This they do day and night. I am starting to lose my identity and to believe that I am all those people they say I am.

Psychiatrist: What roles they force you to be?

Asset: First they say I am to behave as if I was a liquid, then I am to behave as if I was non-liquid?

Psychiatrist: You mean solid?

Asset: No; they insist on the word non-liquid apparently my town

sometimes has a bad smell and for that I assume, although no one told me, I am expected to behave like a gas and disappear into thin air.

Psychiatrist: What other roles they make you perform?

Asset: Well they sometimes ask me to be tangible? They start touching me and undressing me. I am too embarrassed to explain.

Psychiatrist: Any other role?

Asset: Well there is this weird role they make me do; they call me when I am in that role "non- tangible"? I am supposed to be something that people cannot see or touch but are still willing to pay big money for. When I am in this "non –tangible" role I am so confused I usually faint. Can you help me please?

Psychiatrist: I suggest you eat lots of bills of cash, three times a day for six weeks and come back to see me.

Jungle Gym: What are you supposed to teach the children that come to the playground?

Seesaw: That life is all ups and downs.

Jungle Gym: I noticed the other day one fat kid sitting on one side of you, holding up a crying skinnier kid, sitting on your other side. What were you teaching then?

Seesaw: Do not mess around with somebody who is bigger unless you have a plan to defeat him.

Jungle Gym: I also saw the same fat kid, sitting on one side of you, stuck high in the air while five other kids were pushing down on your other side. What was the lesson then?

Seesaw: There is always power in numbers no matter how strong your opponent is.

Jungle Gym: It seems you have quite a lot to teach.

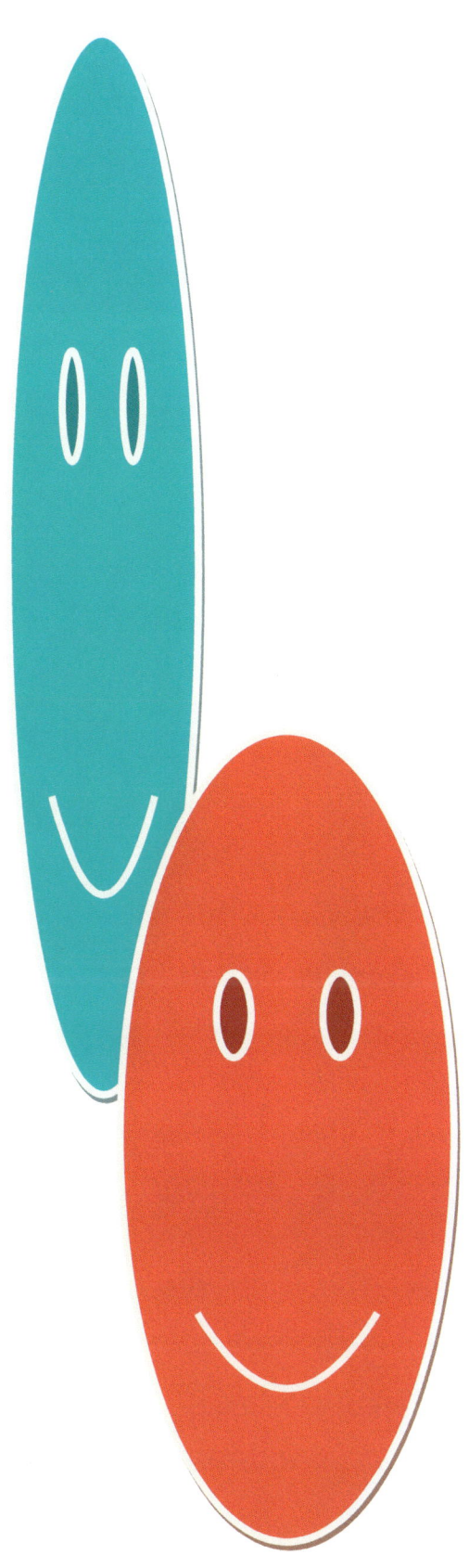

Seesaw: How about you? What is it you are supposed to teach the kids?

Jungle Gym: At first I thought I am supposed to train them to become monkeys.

Seesaw: How about now?

Jungle Gym: Now I know that I am here to create the urge in them to climb to the top.

Seesaw: What happens when they reach there?

Jungle Gym: In my case they learn that there is nothing up there that they could not have got at any of my lower levels.

Seesaw: Do you get paid on the basis of the number of children you teach?

Jungle Gym: No on the basis of the "moan-free" time I provide for their Mothers.

Seesaw: Same here.

Wife: When do you plan to retire?

Husband: When the time is due.

Wife: You mean when you reach a certain age?

Husband: No; age has nothing to do with it.

Wife: But in your company you cannot work beyond a certain age?

Husband: You asked me when I would retire not when I would stop going to my current job.

Wife: You plan to seek another job after you reach the pension age in this one?

Husband: A job in which I have a boss, no; a job in which I am the boss yes.

Wife: But you do not have any capital to start a business? Also you have never shown any inclination to run a business.

Husband: Once again you made an assumption that having a job in which I am my own boss means

running a business. This is not necessary the case.

Wife: You do not want to retire, you do not want a new job after you retire from your current one and you do not want to run your own business, what else is left?

Husband: I am very sad that you think that life is limited by these three options.

Wife: Tell me what other options do you have?

Husband: If at your age you do not know then there is no point in telling you.

Wife: Why not?

Husband: Because to you doing means working; to me it is not.

Wife: You mean doing can be working without pay?

Husband: Yes.

Wife: I do understand; I have been doing it all my life; it's not fun.

Daughter: Dad, do you know the name of the tallest tree in the world?

Father: No I do not.

Daughter: Do you know the name of the second tallest tree in the world?

Father: If I do not know the name of the tallest tree what makes you think I would know the name of the second tallest?

Daughter: It is because of something Mum once said.

Father: What did the fountain of all knowledge say?

Daughter: When I asked her why she married you; she replied that she decided to settle for second best. When I asked why; she replied that it was easier.

Politician: What face should I wear on today?

Assistant: That of a "sympathetic listener"; we are visiting a poor neighbourhood.

Politician: How about Tuesday?

Assistant: It is your "proud non bending hero" face; you are giving a speech at and army barracks.

Politician: What is Wednesday's face?

Assistant: "Reach for the clouds" face; you are at a local school speaking to pupils.

Politician: How about Thursday?

Assistant: "It is your fair reward for a hard day's work" face; you are addressing the local union branch.

Politician: What is Friday's face?

Assistant: It is your "we must be able to compete in the world" face; you are addressing the Association of Machine Manufactures.

Politician: How about Saturday?

Assistant: It your day with your family?

Politician: I know; I am asking you what face should I put on?

Assistant: Oh! I suppose the "caring father and loving husband face"?

Politician: Fine. I will take care of Sunday.

Assistant: How Sir?

Politician: I will put a bag over my head and keep quiet all day.

Assistant: Does that help you?

Politician: No; but it is my way of being charitable on Sunday.

Wife: Why do you want to buy a parrot?

Husband: So he repeats what I say?

Wife: What for?

Husband: To show me how silly I can be in some of things that I say.

Wife: Where will you put it?

Husband: In the sitting room close to the window.

Wife: What happens when I have my usual guests?

Husband: I have no issue that you and your guests also benefit from his services.

Teacher: Why did you pour dirty water on his desk and seat?

Pupil: Because he hit me without any reason?

Teacher: Why did you not come and complain to me? I would have punished him.

Pupil: That's not how we do things at home.

Teacher: Does your father hit you then?

Pupil: No but he hits my Mother.

Teacher: What does your Mother do about it?

Pupil: She and I piss on all the pillows and beds at home after he leaves to work.

Teacher: Has that stopped him hitting her?

Pupil: No; but it stopped him sleeping at home.

Government: Why did you bribe my employee? It is illegal and unethical to do so.

Businessman: I did not bribe him; in any case I have nothing to gain from you by bribing him.

Government: I saw you handing him money; why would you do that if it was not a bribe?

Businessman: That is his winnings from a bet he placed with me.

Government: What bet?

Businessman: When I last met him to complete a transaction I had with you he told me that you have changed the procedures once again and that I need

additional signatures and documents from other departments before he can process my paperwork.

Government: So; I have to improve my controls; what do you expect? Any way I do not see what the bet had to do with that?

Businessman: Your employee made a bet with me that by the time I return to him with the additional documents you have requested you would have changed the procedures once again. I thought you would not have the time; so I bet against him and lost.

Photocopier: I am really sick of you photocopying the same letter every day; why do you keep doing that?

Secretary: But it is the only letter that I have ever received from Mr. Mason.

Photocopier: Who the hell is he?

Secretary: He works in accounts; you know the blond tall guy with a small moustache.

Photocopier: So what is special about him?

Secretary: Are you crazy! All the girls will die to get him to go out with them. He is adorable.

Photocopier: What does the letter say?

Secretary: Who cares; something about me getting a salary cut for daydreaming. The thing is it has his signature on it.

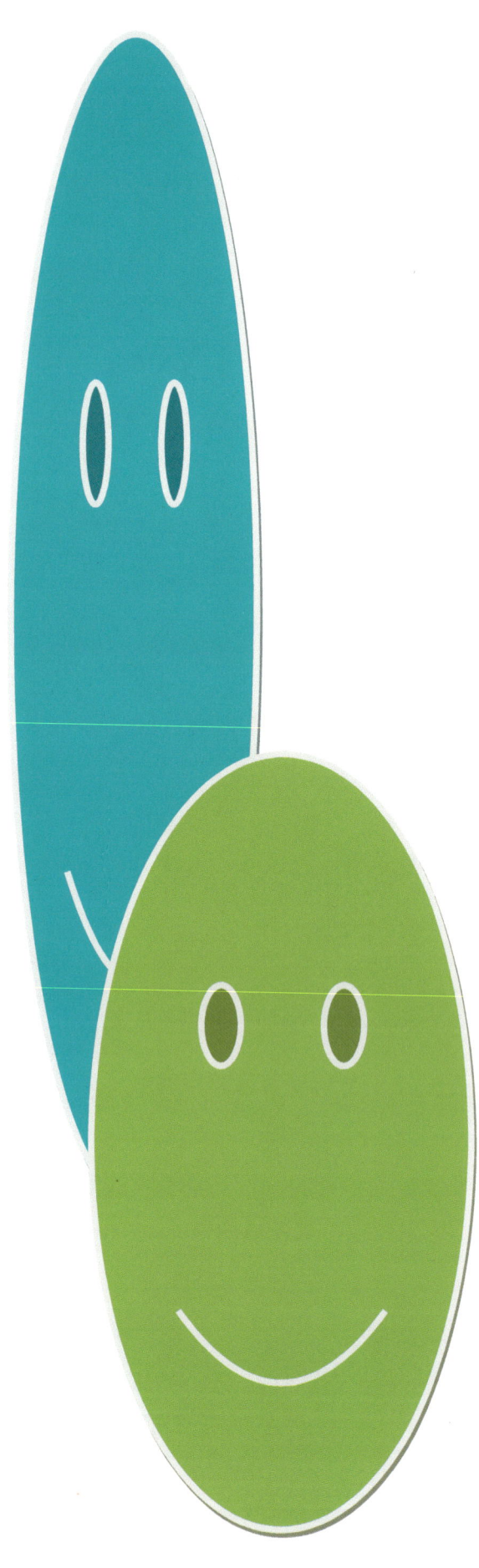

Tourist: I have to leave now.

Inn Keeper: I hope you have enjoyed your stay.

Tourist: Thank you; it was very pleasant.

Inn Keeper: Are you going home?

Tourist: I am always home.

Inn Keeper: You never said where home is?

Tourist: Where respect never sleeps; freedom is always smiling and pride has no price.

Inn Keeper: Where you born there?

Tourist: No I immigrated to it.

Inn Keeper: So it was by choice?

Tourist: Everyone in the Bazaar is there by choice; and anyone who leaves does so by choice.

CPSIA information can be obtained
at www.ICGtesting.com
Printed in the USA
LVIC030018080412
2768LVUK00006BA